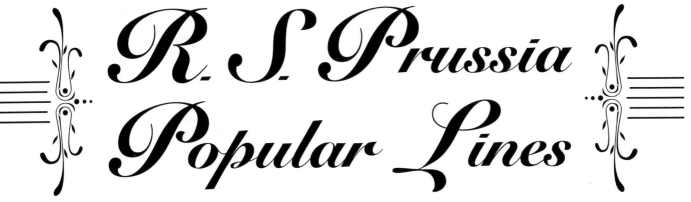

R. S. Prussia Popular Lines

IDENTIFICATION AND VALUE GUIDE

Mary Frank Gaston

COLLECTOR BOOKS

A Division of Schroeder Publishing Co., Inc.

Searching For A Publisher?

We are always looking for knowledgeable people considered experts within their fields. If you feel that there is a real need for a book on your collectible subject and have a large comprehensive collection, contact Collector Books.

On The Cover

Front Cover:
Top Left: Cracker Jar, 7½"h, Mold 644, multi-colored roses, $350.00 – 450.00
Right: Vase, 9¾"h, Mold 939, Cottage scene, $800.00 – 900.00.
Bottom Left: Cracker Jar, 9¼" x 5", Mold 658, pink and white poppies, $350.00 – 450.00.

Back Cover:
Top Left: Cake Plate, 9¾"d, Mold 28, multi-colored roses, $225.00 – 275.00.
Right: Chocolaate Pot, 10½"h, Mold 631, pheasant, $900.00 – 1,000.00.
Bottom Left: Chocolate Pot, 10"h, Mold 628, pink poppies and lilies, $500.00 – 600.00.

Cover photographs courtesy of Barbara and Harold Bragg, John Beck, and David Mullins.

Cover design: Beth Summers
Book layout: Holly C. Long

Collector Books
P.O. Box 3009
Paducah, KY 42002-3009

Printed in the U.S.A. by Image Graphics, Paducah, KY

Contents

Acknowledgments

For this book on R. S. Prussia, I am indebted to all the contributors to the first, second, and third editions. Those titles are now out of print, and I have selected photographs of R. S. Prussia from them for this book. Once, again, I would like to thank the numerous collectors who either permitted me to photograph their collections or sent photographs to me which were printed in those earlier editions and which are included here.

First Series Contributors

Mr. and Mrs. James Baxter, Mt. Vernon, IL
Mr. and Mrs. Bob Feely, Barby Sales, Emmaus, PA
Mrs. Marian L. Fine, Albuquerque, NM
Jessie Hall, Jessie's Showcase of Antiques, Fort Worth, TX
Mr. and Mrs. Ray Hoeppner, New Albany, IN
Imogene Meissner, Imo's Folly, Granbury, TX
Mr. and Mrs. James Sights, House of R. S., Robards, KY
Allen Antiques
Phil Anderson, Anderson's Antiques & Art Gallery, Oklahoma City, OK
Anna Belle's Antiques, Oklahoma City, OK
Joe Bell, Black Gold Antiques, Oklahoma City, OK
Hazel Boggs
Joe and Dolores Broaddus, J & D Antiques, Moro, IL
Glen and Glenda Cooley, Tomorrow's Treasures, Oklahoma City, OK
Kathleen and Jack Cunningham, Pot Luck Antiques, Texarkana, TX
Tom Foster, Tom's Antiques, Tulsa, OK
Marian Gilbert, Decatur, GA
Doris and Harold Hagen, Antique Nook, Las Vegas, NV
Berkley Hunt
Oren and Donna McCaslin, Hogeye Antiques, Phillipsburg, MO
C. R. and Billie McChesnee, Pine Cone Antiques, Arp, TX
Ray and Jean Ludwig, Henderson House Antiques, Henderson, TX
Mannan's Antiques, Indianapolis, IN
Martini's, Las Vegas, NV
Mary's Den of Antiquity, Las Vegas, NV
Laura Lou Medley, Laura's Antiques & Gifts, Oklahoma City, OK
Norm Miller, The Shop Antiques, Salina, KA
Trudy Miller, Dallas, TX
Old Coffee Mill Antiques, Carthage, MO
Olde Towne Antique Mall, Springfield, MO
Jeane Parris, Sugarplums, etc., Las Vegas, NV
Riggs Antiques, Evansville, IN
Ken Roberts, Ken's Antiques, Tulsa OK
Marge Shellabarger, Shellabarger's Antiques, Sullivan, IL
The Yester-Year Mart, Las Vegas, NV
Edward A. Wheeler, Mt. Vernon, IL

Second Series Contributors

Richard Anderson, Beloit, KA
Antique Showcase, Fredricksburg, TX
Mr. and Mrs. Robert Arbuckle
Ron Baldwin and Maxine Baldwin, Cobweb Corner Antiques, Doniphan, NE
Betty and Les Bedore
Robert L. Butikas, Westville, lL
William A. Butikas, Westville, IL
Nancy and Paul Cels, Te Puke, New Zealand
Leonard "Dutch" Chevalier, Memphis, TN
Nancy Clifford, Washington
Rita and Carl Clemons, Mesquite, TX
Mrs. John D. Connell, Dallas, TX
Mrs. Ralph Dickey, Mt. Vernon, IN
Elaine Dopp
Gene Galloway, The Partnership, Dallas, TX
Robert Gollmar, Wisconsin Dells, WI
Ken Harmon
Gene Harris Auctions, Marshalltown, IA
Claire Hohnstein
Dee and Maurice Hooks, Lawrenceville, IL
Maurice L. Hooks, Washington
Mr. and Mrs. L. Edward Huber, Bethlehem, PA
Mrs. Lyman Jeffries
Mrs. Phoebe John, Auckland, New Zealand
Robert V. Larsen Collection
John and Anna Lowe, Sharpsburg, MD
Mrs. J. C. McKelvain, Dallas, TX
Emma McLean
Clarence and Ida Louise Meyer, Fort Scott, KA
Ruth Ann Minderman
Mel Mitchell, The Partnership, Dallas, TX
Barbara Montgomery
Bill Moss, Memphis, TN
Marti Owens
Dee Reed, Ohio
Henry G. and Edna M. Reed, Ft. Worth, TX
Don and Irene Reeves, Fairmount, IN
Edward S. Rutowski, Erie PA
Ralph and Eunice Schlegelmilch, Lancaster, PA
Virginia Schofner, Clearwater, FL
T. Schwalbach, WI

Donna Smith, Yreka, CA
Mrs. George Stever, Sunnyvale, CA
Edward and Pamela Wolfe
Woody Auctions, Douglass, KA

Third Series Contributors

Martha and Robert R. Allen, Manns Harbor, NC
Charles and Karen Aschenbeck, Houston, TX
Helen Bailey, Kirksville, MO
Lawrence and Judith Bazaar
John Becker, Columbus, OH
John and Bea Bell
Rose Ellen and Walt Beyer, Omaha, NE
Edda Biesterfield, Bonn, Germany
Merle N. Blanton, Mechanicsburg, OH
Phyllis Boege, Richton Park, IL
Kerry and Christine Bottcher, Bowmanstown, PA
Dale R. Bowser, Brookville, OH
Freda Bradford
Harold and Barbara Bragg, OH
Noreen and R. H. Capers, Fort Meade, MD
Suzan Cartwright
Richard and Florence Chaney, Myrtle Creek, OR
Nancy J. Clifford, WA
Frances and Terry Coy, Louisville, KY
Phillip Crutcher, Moberly, MO
Edna M. Dennie
Mrs. Ralph Dickey, Mt. Vernon, IN
Sharon Dollos, DuQuoin, IL
Lavaine Donovan
Mike Edgar
Patty Erickson
Margie Fowler, Warrenton, MO
Ken and Debra Fuelberth, IL
Gloria and Byman Geyer, Mansfield, TX
Doris and Carl Gibbs, San Antonio, TX
Nancy Glass, Germantown, TN
John and Sharon Gold, Easton, PA
Robert Gollmar, Rochester, WI
Marian E. Gordon, OH
Nash and Jeannie Hayes, Lebanon, KY
Cynthia Helping, West Milton, OH
John and Deanna Hill, Forest City, IA
Claire Hohnstein

Peter Hohnstein and Deb Schark, Robinson, IL
Maurice and Dee Hooks, Lawrenceville, IL
Maurice L. Hooks, WA
David W. Irwin, Jr.
Nancy A. Jensen, WI
Jody's Antiques, Antique World Mall, North Little Rock, AR
Lee Kirkpatrick
Delbert Krug, Solon, IA
John Law, Fort Dodge, IA
Carl and Phyllis Leohr
Paul Linden, Bellville, WI
Rich and Priscilla Lindstrom, St. Joseph, IL
Debbie Lobel, Arlington, TX
Dr. and Mrs. Wm. J. Luke, Scottsdale, AR
Mary and Robert McCaslin, Danville, IN
Clarence and Ida Meyer, Fort Scott, KS
Marlene and Gene Miller, IN
David Mullins, Columbus, OH
Hoy and Virginia Mullins, WV
Byron Murray
Robert Pompilio, Garden City, NY
Irene Reeves, Alexandria, IN
Kevin Reiman
Jean Riecker, Northville, MI
The Rileys of Ohio
Dale and Amber Rothrock
Tom Rouch, Pierston, IN
Lucille Rowoldt
Barbara and Shelby Smith, Muncie, IN
Donald South
Mr. and Mrs. Oscar Srp, Dayton, OH
Adam Stein, III, High Point, NC
Arlo Stender, Cumberland, IA
Thomas Surratt
Janelle and Gordon Sweeter
Yvonne L. Titchener
Mr. and Mrs. Gary Thomas, Alexandria, IN
Cheryl and Tim van der Hagen, MN
Judy White, Kalamazoo, MI
Joyce and Jack Williams, Irvine, CA
Bonnie and John Willis, El Dorado Hills, CA
Frank Wine, Jr., Portsmouth, VA
Pam Wolfe
Woody Auctions, Douglass, KA
Pete and Viola Zwern, Denver, CO

Preface

R. S. Prussia porcelain enjoys an enthusiastic popularity among porcelain collectors. Since my first book on the subject was published in 1982, collectors have continually wanted to know more about the factories which made the china and the production of those factories. Such a demand for information led to my Second, Third, and Fourth Series.

In my first book, I presented a Mold Identification system for R. S. Prussia pieces. Today, those Mold ID Numbers are used extensively by collectors to describe particular pieces they have or wish to purchase. Auction houses describe pieces by the numbers in their catalogs, and antique price guides refer to the numbers in their listings under Schlegelmilch China or R. S. Prussia.

In the Second Series published in 1986, I expanded the Mold ID System. A variety of new molds were introduced as well as different objects and different decorations for molds previously shown in the first book. I also included a number of different marks from the ones illustrated in the first edition. New information, based on several German references, regarding which factories had used the R. S. Prussia mark was discussed.

I thought surely that with these two books the subject was covered. But I was wrong! Collectors wrote describing more marks, new molds, different decorations, and R. S. marked pieces for molds previously only found as unmarked. The most impressive information, however, came from a collector with whom I had corresponded for several years. Ron Capers was stationed in Germany in the 1980s, and while there, he and his wife, Noreen, began collecting R. S. Prussia and Schlegelmilch china. He was in Germany in 1990 when the Berlin Wall fell, and he was able to travel to Suhl, the city where the Schlegelmilch factories were founded. He discovered a manuscript written in 1984 by Bernd Hartwich about the factories. Being fluent in German, Capers translated the manuscript, and furnished me and the International Association of R. S. Prussia Collectors, Inc. a copy. This manuscript greatly clarified the history of the Schlegelmilch factories, bringing out new information presented in my Third Series in 1994. Caper's book, *Caper's Notes on the Marks of Prussia*, was published in 1996. In addition to showing a comprehensive survey of the many marks used by the companies and examples of those marks, the book also discusses the history of the factories and other interesting material about the Schlegelmilch families. His book is recommended for all collectors and is listed in my Bibliography.

In addition to new historical information presented in the Third Series, I introduced an Index to Floral

Transfer Designs found on R. S. Prussia china. One hundred patterns were listed and described in a chart, and the "FD" numbers were used in the photograph descriptions. Only R. S. Prussia china was included in that edition.

Pieces with other R. S. marks and examples by other Schlegelmilch factories such as Erdmann, Oscar, and Carl Schlegelmilch were shown in my Fourth Series, released in 1995. A special section illustrated unmarked china and ambiguously marked china such as "Royal Vienna" and "Saxe Altenburg." While some molds and decorations of such china may match R. S. Prussia marked molds and decorations, certain molds and decorations often appear to be unique to those ambiguous marks or are only found on unmarked china. Floral transfers and molds were identified for the pieces shown. Collectors interested in other R. S. marks and examples such as R. S. Germany, R. S. Suhl, and R. S. Poland, as well as E. S. (Erdmann Schlegelmilch), O. S. (Oscar Schlegelmilch), and C. S. (Carl Schlegelmilch) china, are referred to in the Fourth Series.

The First, Second, and Third editions of my books on R. S. Prussia are currently out of print. I am happy to say that most collectors have all of these books. But for new collectors as well as advanced collectors, I have written this new edition. A survey of R. S. Prussia incorporating examples from all of my previous three books presents the best of the best, so to speak.

This book focuses on R. S. Prussia china made by the Reinhold Schlegelmilch factories in Suhl and Tillowitz. The first chapter presents the company's history. This material has been reprinted from the Third Series, but includes revised historical data not only for the Reinhold Schlegelmilch factories but also information for the other three companies. It is important for collectors, especially beginners, to be aware of the new information for all Schlegelmilch companies in order to gain a clear perspective on the subject.

In my other books, the study of R. S. Prussia pieces has centered around mold identification. This edition takes a different approach by using the many themes of decoration to group the pictures. In the First Series, I wrote about decoration on porcelain in general and on R. S. Prussia specifically. That information has been reprinted here in chapter 2.

This new edition illustrates only R. S. Prussia examples. Chapter 3 shows six variations of the R. S. Prussia wreath and star mark. The particular mark number is not indicated in the captions of the pictures unless there is some particular variation. If an example is not marked, that information is noted in the caption.

Pictures are shown according to decoration subject. Within each decoration category, pieces are arranged by specific mold. Unlike the lay-out used in my earlier books, all pieces in a mold, whether they are horizontal, vertical, or accessory items and have different mold numbers, are shown together. For example, Plates, Bowls, Pitchers, Mustard Jars, and Vases with the same decoration for a mold such as Mold 25, the Iris Mold, are grouped together. It is interesting to see R. S. Prussia arranged in this manner. We can see which molds were used for certain decorations. Sometimes a variety of molds was used for the same decoration transfer, but it is apparent that some decorations are found primarily on just a few molds. Arrangement by decoration enables us also to see how the same floral transfer may look quite different when placed on different molds and different pieces.

In the Second Series, I discussed in the Preface to the Value Guide decorations on R. S. Prussia which were considered popular, scarce, or rare. Please note that decorations can be both popular and prevalent, and popular and rare or scarce. In chapter 4, I present pieces which not only have popular decorations but decorations which are quite prevalent and found readily on the market. This section contains popular figural, portrait, scenic, and bird decorations. Some of these are the Melon Eaters, the Four Seasons, Madame LeBrun, Cottage Scene, and Swans. The original works of art on which some of these transfers were based were discussed in my first book. That information and other comments relating to each transfer are included for each decoration.

Chapter 5 looks at floral transfers found on R. S. Prussia china. The floral designs are the most prevalent of all decorations, and this section contains numerous examples. I have selected what I consider the most popular floral designs from the 100 I listed in the Third Series. A brief description of the floral transfer heads each sub-category.

Other popular decorations can be classified as scarce or even rare. These examples are shown in chapter 6. The Fruit transfers, for instance, are scarce compared to the Four Seasons or Swans. Napoleon is more often found on ES-marked china rather than R. S. Prussia, and thus is a scarce portrait decoration. The Masted Ships are examples of scarce scenic designs. Admiral Peary scenes, jungle animals, and exotic birds are considered to be rare decorations. Few examples surface and when they do, collectors are quick to seek them. Those decorations are both rare and popular and command the very highest price.

Finally, this book could not be complete, regrettably, without a section on reproductions. The fake R. S. Prussia marks and misleading R. S. marks with examples which are shown in my Fourth Series are reprinted here in chapter 7. The fake R. S. Suhl mark and examples are also included because the same new pieces may be found with a fake or misleading R. S. Prussia mark as well.

The value range for each piece is listed in the caption of each photograph. Additionally, for collector interest and convenience, three Appendices from the Third Series have been reprinted: the Mold Identification Chart; the Floral Identification Chart; and Creative Artists' Signatures. Indexes for Decoration Subjects and Objects are also included.

I hope you enjoy this new edition, *R. S. Prussia Popular Lines.*

Chapter 1

Revised Historical Origins of the Schlegelmilch Porcelain Factories

Suhl and Mäbendorf
Langewiesen
Tillowitz

Suhl and Mäbendorf

Suhl, the town where the Schlegelmilch porcelain factories originated, has an intricate and varied history as part of the Germanic region of Thuringia. The town had been under different rulers from feudal times until, as a result of the Treaty of Vienna enacted on May 22, 1815, it became a part of the region acquired by the German state of Prussia. Hartwich (1984: 2) describes the town after that date as "...a part of the County of Schleusingen, Prussian District of Erfurt, Provine of Saxony." It is interesting to note that several names mentioned here, "Suhl," "Thuringia," "Prussia," and "Saxony," are all words which can be found in marks on Schlegelmilch china.

The foundation of Suhl as a center for porcelain production was the result of the town's earlier iron ore industry. That business was described as being at its peak during the sixteenth century. It led, in fact, to the development of weapons manufacturing as well in Suhl during that time. Over the next 300 years, the iron ore was depleted, and mining for the mineral had ceased in Suhl by the end of the 1800s. The forges in Suhl needed to be converted to other uses. It was discovered that those forges could be adapted to manufacturing porcelain (Hartwich, 1984: 3).

True porcelain had been made in Germany since about 1708. Historically, the discovery of the technique in the Western world has been attributed to Johann Fredrich Böttger, an alchemist of Meissen. His work led to the founding of the Royal Meissen Porcelain Company. The secret of making true porcelain was guarded for many years. Over time, however, the knowledge was carried to other regions in Germany as well as to other countries by workers going from one area to another. Porcelain factories, other than Meissen, were operating in Germany under royal patronage during the middle 1700s.

Twelve porcelain factories were established in Thuringia during the early period of the industry's development in Germany from about 1760 until 1800, beginning with the Sitzendorf and Volkstedt factories (Hartwich, 1984: 4). During the 1800s, private ownership of porcelain factories became possible. Thus, the way was open for individuals to start their own china factories. It is not surprising that two people in Suhl decided to try their hand at this particular business.

Three porcelain factories under the name of Schlegelmilch were actually put into production after 1860. This occurred about 100 years after the Sitzendorf and Volkstedt factories were established in Thuringia. According to Hartwich (1984: 6, 19, 27), the Erdmann Schlegelmilch Factory was founded in 1861; the Reinhold Schlegelmilch Factory was founded in 1869, and the Carl Schlegelmilch factory was founded in 1882. While these same dates are really not new information to collectors, the family relationship between the owners of the E.S. and R.S. factories is not what has previously been thought.

The name "Schlegelmilch" is a common Germanic one, especially for the area where the factories were located. While there may have been some connection between Reinhold's and Erdmann's families, the two were not brothers. They did not have a father named "Rudolph," nor was the famous "R.S." trademark symbolic of his name as stated by C. Schlegelmilch (1970: 16). According to a genealogical study of the family which was made by R. H. Capers between 1990 and 1992, Erdmann and Reinhold apparently came from two separate families. The name "Rudolph," in fact, does not appear in any of the historical documents found pertaining to either the Erdmann Schlegelmilch or Reinhold Schlegelmilch families. The Reinhold Schlegelmilch family tree, which resulted from this research, is shown in the Third Series. Erdmann Schlegelmilch's family tree is in the Fourth Series.

The origins of the three Schlegelmilch porcelain factories in Suhl are discussed in the following sections under separate headings. The information is largely based on the 1984 Hartwich study as translated by R. H. Capers.

The Erdmann Schlegelmilch Factory

Perhaps the most interesting new fact concerning the factories is that the ES factory was not founded by Erdmann Schlegelmilch. It was established by his sons: Leonhard, Carl August, and Friedrich Wilhelm (Hartwich, 1984: 8). Carl August, the oldest son, inherited an iron forge when Erdmann died in 1844. Events of the mid 1800s, such as the lack of iron ore and high mining costs associated with trying to extract the remaining ore, caused forge owners to close their businesses or look for alternative uses for the plants and equipment. The Schlegelmilch brothers "experimentally converted in 1861, under the management of Leonhard Schlegelmilch, a part of their forge for the manufacture of porcelain" (Hartwich, 1984: 8). It is necessary to stress the word "experimentally." Evidently, there was not any large scale porcelain production at first. This may explain, in part, why information on dating the various E.S. marks cannot be traced to those years of the early 1860s and 1870s.

The forge could be converted to porcelain production because it already had gas, glazing, and drying furnaces. The same type of equipment is also necessary for firing china. Leonhard, manager of the factory, is described by Hartwich (1984: 10) as using all means to persuade workers from other porcelain factories in the area to leave their jobs and come to work for him. We are told that Leonhard was trained as a sculptor at the Art Academy in Düsseldorf. Consequently, his first production of porcelain was geared to artistic wares. Because of stiff competition in that line of items from longer established factories, the ES factory turned its production to more utilitarian ware (Hartwich, 1984: 10). The porcelain factory was named for the brothers' father, Erdmann. Once a marking system was implemented, the marks incorporated his initials or even his full name.

The production of the factory was intended for the export trade. The range of items made was quite varied, consisting largely of table china and decorative accessories. The company's efforts evidently met with success, because over the years the iron forge was completely turned over to porcelain manufacturing. The factory exported not only to England and the United States, but it also shipped china to France, Italy, and Russia. The business experienced cyclical ups and downs over the years during the 1870s and 1880s as the economic circumstances of the export countries fluctuated. The raising of tariffs by these countries was the major hardship for the factory.

The management of the ES factory also changed over time. In 1881 Leonhard placed his son Carl, from his first marriage, in charge of the business. In 1882 Julius Martin Schlegelmilch, Leonhard's son from a second marriage, took over the management of the company. In 1885 another son from Leonhard's first marriage, Oscar, joined Julius Martin in becoming partners with their father in the business (Hartwich, 1984: 12).

During the late 1880s the ES factory continued to expand its facilities. Increased tariffs by the United States for imported china effectively closed that source as a market, however. Consequently, on September 1, 1891, the partnership established in 1885 ended, and Julius Schlegelmilch became the sole owner of the company. His half brother, Oscar, went to another town, Langewiesen (also in Thuringia), in 1882 and established his own factory. Leonhard died in 1898 at the age of 74 (Hartwich, 1984: 13).

Tariffs for importing china into the United States were dramatically reduced in 1894 with the implementation of the Wilson Customs Bill. As a result, the ES factory was able to take advantage of the situation. Business was so good that the plant was expanding once again. The "boom" was short-lived, however, because the McKinley Tariff Bill was enacted in 1896. That bill brought back the higher duties on china imported to the United States. Local conditions in Suhl, such as increased freight and coal prices, as well as the Japanese entry into the American china market after 1891 were other factors which led to the decline of the company during the late 1890s. Although Julius Schlegelmilch tried to maintain his production, even continuing to expand and remodel his facilities during 1898 and 1899, it was necessary to reorganize the company on December 14, 1899. At that time it was converted to a joint stock company with Julius retaining control by ownership of the largest number of shares (Hartwich, 1984: 14).

The early years of the twentieth century saw the rise and fall of the company again. The problems were basically the same as in the other years: United States tariffs, Japanese competition, and rising domestic costs for coal and other supplies needed for making china. In 1906 the joint stock company organized in 1899 declared bankruptcy with the result that the company was dissolved on January 31, 1908 (Hartwich, 1984: 15). However, the company was re-registered on Feb. 8, 1908. Attempts were once more initiated to keep the factory in production. Facilities again were expanded and improved. Increased American tariffs coupled with the beginning of World War I caused the company to drastically reduce its production. The lucrative overseas markets were closed to the company, and workers were drafted into the military. The factory was taken over by the Berlin War Office in 1917 (Hartwich, 1984: 16).

After the end of World War I, the company was again able to recover and re-enter the export market. The business enjoyed another expansion not only in workers but also in the increased variety of items manufactured. But as with the pre-war years, conditions soon developed from which the company was finally unable to recover. The problems centered in 1922 on the local high German inflation, causing orders to fall. Obviously with fewer orders, production had to be reduced over the next several years. The work week was limited to four days in 1926, and the work force was cut by one third (Hartwich, 1984: 17). All these factors resulted in escalated costs for manufacturing. The high costs of coal and raw materials as well as increased tariffs, not only in America but also in England, combined to create too large an obstacle for the company to overcome. The worldwide Depression of the 1930s was the final blow for the business. Hartwich (1984: 17) notes:

In 1930, 250 workers were still employed, but by October/December 1931, only 116 remained. Starting in January 1931, no more orders came in; therefore, the number of workers decreased further so that in October/December 1933, only 79 workers were still employed...In the Summer of 1935, the Erdmann Schlegelmilch porcelain factory closed down... In the next two years, the factory facilities and buildings were sold. On 10 April 1937, the Erdmann Schlegelmilch Porcelain Factory Open Trading Company was stricken from the Trade Register in Suhl.

Marks and photographs of the Erdmann Schlegelmilch Company are covered in the Fourth Series.

The Reinhold Schlegelmilch Factory

Hartwich (1984: 19) states that in 1868, Reinhold Schlegelmilch purchased a forge which had been owned by Kaspar Schlegelmilch since 1856. However, no family relationship is mentioned between Reinhold and Kaspar. It is also mentioned that Carl August Schlegelmilch, Erdmann's son, was co-owner of the forge; however, his part was also bought out by Reinhold.

Reinhold purchased the forge for the purpose of

establishing a porcelain factory. The name of the enterprise became "Reinhold Schlegelmilch." The company was formally registered in Suhl on October 24, 1869 (Hartwich, 1984: 19). The factory soon became the largest in the area, especially overshadowing the Erdmann Schlegelmilch factory. After 10 years, Reinhold's factory employed more than twice the number of workers at the ES factory. The production of the two potteries was similar; chiefly, table wares were manufactured for the export trade.

In the 1870s and early 1880s Reinhold continued to expand his facilities. His company did not suffer from the external tariffs and local economic situations of that period as much as the ES Company. The reason for this, Hartwich (1984: 20) explains, is because Reinhold's interests were diversified. For example, he owned cattle which enabled him to have a means of transportation for his raw materials and finished manufactured goods between Suhl and Grimmenthal, the closest railhead. There was no rail line in Suhl until 1882. Transportation in and out of the local area was thus a major concern.

Severe restrictions of the American McKinley Tariff of 1896, however, did affect Reinhold's company. Prices for his china fell, but he continued to hire more workers and enlarge his factory over the next several years. The factory during this time is said to have produced only "staple commodities" because they not only sold well but could also be easily stored (Hartwich, 1984: 20). This would presumably be a source of supply to be sold at a later time when conditions were better.

Hartwich (1984: 20) states, "On 12 October 1886 (Reinhold) gave the business procuration to his brother, the merchant, Otto Schlegelmilch, and on 17 December 1887, to his brother, Ehrhard Schlegelmilch." The term "business procuration" is interpreted as meaning that the person so named was brought into the company to actively take part in the business. Note that while Hartwich says "Ehrhard" was Reinhold's brother, research on the family tree indicates that he was Reinhold's son. This makes sense if one looks at the date of birth for Ehrhard. Reinhold was born in 1837, and Ehrhard was born in 1866. These dates were on the graves found in Tillowitz in 1992. It should be pointed out that Ehrhard may be spelled in several different ways, such as "Erhard," "Erhardt," "Ehrhardt," and "Ehrhard." From this point on the name will be spelled "Erhard."

The Reinhold Schlegelmilch factory in Suhl grew larger and larger from the late 1880s through the 1890s. The 1893 Coburg Ceramic Directory lists showrooms for the company in Amsterdam, Berlin, Bucharest, Constantinople, and Hamburg. It was shown to have had 500 employees. The company built facilities such as housing and shops for its workers, becoming a type of "company town." In 1894 the owners of the factory were registered as Reinhold Schlegelmilch and Arnold Schlegelmilch (Reinhold's son) in Suhl, and Erhard Schlegelmilch in Tillowitz (Hartwich, 1984: 21).

As for the ES Company, the easing of the American duty restrictions of the Wilson Tariff in 1894 made it possible for the RS factory in Suhl to export more china to the United States. This resulted in a few more profitable years for the business, but the reprieve did not last long as higher tariffs were once more imposed with the McKinley Bill of 1896. This, together with the increased Japanese competition for the American market, was very detrimental to the factory. Attempts were made to modernize the facility by introducing electricity as a source of energy. The plant was enlarged again as well. Local conditions also worked against the company because raw materials for making the china as well as coal had to be brought in from outside the local area. Rail costs for such transportation were very expensive.

Reinhold Schlegelmilch died on February 19, 1906 (Hartwich, 1984: 23). The date of his death is one of interest to collectors, because it is much earlier than suggested by Clifford Schlegelmilch (1970: 34). He mentions that there was correspondence from Reinhold Schlegelmilch to his (Clifford's) mother in January of 1929: a portion of the letterhead with the date is shown on page 14 of his book. A signature of "Reinhold Schlegelmilch" is also shown; supposedly it is from the letter (the letter was not reproduced). It is obvious that Reinhold's date of death and this signature from 1929 are in conflict. The explanation is probably that the company used the name "Reinhold Schlegelmilch" in correspondence after his death, even as a signature, based on the name of the company. This may have been a common practice, because a letter from the Erdmann Schlegelmilch Factory has "Erdmann Schlegelmilch" as a signature. He had died before the factory was even established.

Reinhold's death occurred some years prior to World War I. Production in the factory began slowing down some years after his death. Only 300 workers are listed for the company by the Coburg Ceramic Directory of 1910. The factory was still able to operate on a limited scale during the first years of the war. It suffered the same problems as the ES factory, however, namely lack of orders and lack of workers. The employees were either being drafted or going to work for the weapon manufacturers.

Arnold, as head of the Suhl factory during those years, made a plea to the Board of Trade in Erfurt on September 18, 1915, that he be allowed to keep at least five skilled workers so that the factory could be put in operation again when the war was over. If this did not occur, Arnold stated "...I will have to shut down my company completely, would never re-open and would be forced to transfer the entire factory to Tillowitz in Upper Silesia." (Hartwich, 1984: 23)

Arnold's plea was not granted, and thus the Reinhold Schlegelmilch factory in Suhl closed in December 1917. It was then relocated in Tillowitz.

The Carl Schlegelmilch Factory

Very little information is known regarding the third Schlegelmilch china factory which was located in Mäbendorf, a suburb of Suhl. This business was started by Carl Schlegelmilch, Leonard's son by his first marriage (Leonhard was Erdmann's son). Carl became the owner of the Mäbendorf Forge in 1882. Evidently, he left his father's business, the ES factory, to start another china manufacturing outlet in the area. He was the only owner of that company until 1912. At that time, it became an open trade company under the name "Mäbendorf Porcelain Factory, Schlegelmilch & Co." Three people (various ES relations) became partners with Carl; they included Carl's half brother, Julius Martin, who was also in charge of the ES factory. That partnership lasted for less than one year because records indicate that Carl Schlegelmilch was once again the only owner on May 27, 1913. The business procuration was given to Carl's son, Hans, on that same day. But Hans was replaced by Carl's wife, Klara, on December 18, 1918, presumably after Carl's death. The company was closed on June 15, 1919. The Carl Schlegelmilch Company was succeeded by Richard Matthes & Co. (Hartwich, 1984: 27, 28).

The only marks shown in references for the Carl Schlegelmilch factory are ones under the name of Mäbendorf, or Matthes & Co., or Matthes & Ebel, the successor to Matthes & Co. With the exception of one mark, the marks are dated from the late 1920s or 1930s. The marks all include the name "Mäbendorf." None of the marks, including one from 1910, incorporates the name "Schlegelmilch" or the initials "C.S."

China is sometimes found in this country, however, which is marked with "C.S. Prussia" under a clover leaf. The china is similar in style and floral decor to some of the china made by the ES factory. Röntgen (1980: 81) and others have attributed this particular mark to Oscar Schlegelmilch. They have evidently mistaken the "C." for an "O." This mark was noted in my first edition (Gaston, 1980: 26) as an unidentified mark. It will now be attributed to the Carl Schlegelmilch factory based on the information that the company existed from 1882.

The lack of many examples with this mark indicates that little was exported to the United States. The mark also may not have been used for very long. It is even possible that in the beginning, the factory did not mark its china, or that it was used as a branch of the ES factory. Alternatively, the factory could have used some mark which has not to date been documented for the company, or it could have used one of the ambiguous marks which are found on pieces which resemble ES or RS china, but which cannot be definitely attributed to either factory. Perhaps more information on this company prior to the 1920s will become available.

Marks and photographs of the Carl Schlegelmilch Company are covered in the Fourth Series.

Langewiesen

Oscar Schlegelmilch was Leonhard Schlegelmilch's son by his first marriage, and thus Erdmann Schlegelmilch's grandson. Oscar was not Reinhold's and Erdmann's nephew as stated by Clifford Schlegelmilch (1970: 16).

There is relatively little historical information available concerning the development of the O. S. Company. We saw that from 1885 until 1891 Oscar had been a partner with his brother and father in the Erdmann Schlegelmilch Factory in Suhl. Oscar left the ES company and moved to Langewiesen which was also in Thuringia. Bad economic conditions for the ES factory probably caused Oscar to leave Suhl. Perhaps he thought he could be more prosperous if he had his own factory. Of course, there could have also been some family disagreement which led to his relocation.

The OS factory apparently was able to succeed while the ES company was failing. The OS porcelain works appear to have been continuously in business from 1892 until 1972. At that time, the factory became a part of the state-owned VEB Porcelain Combine Colditz in Colditz (Röntgen, 1980: 436).

The scarcity of OS-marked china on the American market supports the theory that little of the production was exported to the United States. Thus, the source of the company's success was not dependent on the large American market. It may have depended more on the local area or the closer European countries. The 1910 Coburg Ceramic Directory notes that the factory employed 300 people. Evidently, it was not a small organization. Table wares and decorative items were produced. The transfer decoration was quite similar to that used by the ES factory.

Marks and photographs for the Oscar Schlegelmilch Company are included in the Fourth Series.

Tillowitz

Reinhold Schlegelmilch's factory in Tillowitz, Upper Silesia, was not established in 1869 as has been reported by most references on the subject. Misinformation from unknown sources at some point in time has been the reason why this erroneous date has been perpetuated. The 1869 date merely reflects the founding of Reinhold's first factory which was located in Suhl. This type of misinformation regarding the founding dates for potteries is not uncommon. Often the date when a certain company produced china is listed as the founding date for a much later company who bought the older one or who purchased the plant where china had once been made. Or, in this case and others, the time when a company first started business is used as the founding date for successive operations of that company. Evidently this was a method of adding age and prestige to a later company's production.

Hartwich (p. 23) says that the Reinhold Schlegelmilch factory in Tillowitz had been in business since 1894. The Schlegelmilchs, however, were in Tillowitz prior to 1894. Erhard, Reinhold's son, is noted to have been connected with another pottery in that town about 1887 or 1888. The name of that company was the Graf Frankenberg'sche Factory, noted as originating in the early 1850s. Information from some post World War II refugee newspaper articles described Erhard as working for several years at the Graf Frankenberg'sche Factory before he decided to build his own factory. The Coburg Ceramic Directory of 1893 lists Erhard as director of that factory.

At some point, Erhard decided the Graf Frankenberg'sche Factory needed to expand, but the owners did not agree. Therefore, Erhard, with the backing of his father Reinhold, built a factory in Suhl for the Schlegelmilchs in Tillowitz in 1894. The plant was described as being ready for production in 1895. The factory was located directly on a rail line, making it convenient for bringing in supplies and sending out the finished products. It even had its own rail spur.

The Schlegelmilchs purchased the Graf Frankenberg'sche factory about 1905, because they saw it as competition for their own business. The factory was under the Schlegelmilchs' ownership until 1919 when it was closed and the buildings were turned into apartments. Two marks are noted as having been used by the Graf Frankenberg'sche factory. One is a shield, and the other incorporates the figure of a horse within a double circle. "Tillowitz" is printed inside the double circle. Such marks do not appear to have any connection with the marks used on china by the Schlegelmilch factory they built in Tillowitz. In fact, Wenke (1984: 1) states that the first mark used by the Schlegelmilch factory in Tillowitz was the steeple mark. The initials "S" and "T" on either side of a church reflected the company's two locations in Suhl and Tillowitz.

Opening a second factory in 1895 in Tillowitz was indeed fortuitous for Reinhold Schlegelmilch. When it became necessary to close the Suhl factory during World War I, the Tillowitz plant was still able to produce. It was available, also, to absorb any left-over stock from the Suhl factory. Moreover, we find that the freight costs were much lower in Tillowitz, the raw materials were closer, and the workers could be hired for much smaller wages.

The Tillowitz factory was quite successful in its production and export during its initial years of operation. Like the Suhl factory, the export trade, especially to the United States, was its mainstay. The factory was enlarged early on, and it benefitted from the expertise of some of the best technicians, painters, and mold makers. Several had previously worked at Suhl. It is interesting to note that some names occasionally found as signatures on the faces of R. S. Prussia marked items can now be matched to the individuals who were either mold makers or painters for the company. (See the next section for the names of these artisans.)

Hartwich (p. 24) says that 1897 was the peak year of business for the RS factories. Economic conditions and the competition from the weapons industry for workers are cited as reasons for the slowdown in production in Suhl after that time. Records relating to the Tillowitz factory show that Otto Schlegelmilch joined Arnold, Erhard, and Reinhold as a partner in the company in 1895. In 1922 the company owners were listed as Erhard and Arnold. Arnold had moved to Tillowitz after the Suhl factory closed around 1917. He is credited with developing an ivory porcelain for the company after that time (Pattloch, nd: 1). This would have been a type of china similar to the English bone china which has some translucency but is not considered true porcelain.

The company's prosperity during its early years is shown by the buildings the company had erected for the town. Those included a Lutheran church and school, a sports hall, and housing for the employees. The workers were paid in gold and silver coins, and the china produced was described as being the "peak of German workmanship" (Pattloch, nd: 1). The company exported its china to many other countries besides the U. S.; Australia, the Balkans, England, Holland, Indonesia, Scandinavia, and Switzerland composed part of the market as well. The Coburg Ceramic Address Book of 1910 lists showrooms for the factory in Amsterdam, Hamburg, New York City, Paris, and Vienna. The 1913 directory shows that the company had 600 employees; the 1930 directory lists representatives for the company in Berlin, Cologne, Freiburg, and Dresden.

A newspaper article written in 1938 ("Porzellan Kommt aus OS") described how the factory catered to the artistic tastes of the individual countries which imported Schlegelmilch china. The English were said to like elaborate forms and decorations, and Americans wanted complicated shapes and designs. The Dutch preferred a stronger china. The German market was partial to gold trim and did not care for the intricate forms and decorations which were so popular with the English and American markets. Another article (Warzecha) written in the 1950s explained why Schlegelmilch china was so thin; the American tariffs on imported china were based on weight, thus the thinner the china, the lower the duty.

We know that the world wars divided by the world Depression of the 1930s were contributing factors which caused the Schlegelmilch china business in Tillowitz to ebb and flow over that time. Where the company was listed as having 600 employees in 1910, the force had been reduced to 400 by 1930, according to the Coburg Ceramic Directory of that year. Erhard, the founder of the Tillowitz factory, and his brother, Arnold, both died in 1934. The control of the company was turned over to Arnold's sons, Herbert and Lothar. Hartwich (p. 23) states that Lothar was the sole owner of the factory in 1941, but his date of death was actually on November 6, 1940. At any rate, after Lothar's death the ownership of the company was inherited by Brigitte Koch, the daughter of Christa Koch, Arnold's daughter, and thus Reinhold's great-granddaughter.

In spite of the tumultuous years of the 1920s through the 1940s, the Tillowitz factory was able to stay in business until 1945. During World War II the company also made a type of ware which was called "canteen" china. It was a heavier product, similar to what we might call "hotel" china, not the fine, translucent porcelain made by the company prior to the war. The final day of production of the factory was January 23, 1945 (Soppa, 1991). The owner, Brigitte Koch, fled Tillowitz in 1945 before the factory came under the administration of the Poles. She died in Hamburg in August 1991. The Schlegelmilch family was never able to reclaim their property in Tillowitz.

I described in my first edition (Gaston, 1980: 22) the events which caused the town of Tillowitz to come under the administration of Poland during 1945 at the end of World War II. The factory was kept open under Polish administration. One article notes that this was possible because some of the former workers who did not manage to leave the area before it was occupied were given the task of getting the factory back into production. However, this took well over a year to accomplish, which would have been some time in 1947. The china items made by the factory after that time are described as looking " ...exactly like those from the time of the Schlegelmilch family" (Pattloch, nd: 1).

The reason for this similarity, however, is probably due to old stock being re-marked or double marked with the R.S. Germany mark or a new mark affixed to previously made unmarked stock. That new mark was the "Made in (German) Poland" mark, reflecting the status of the area which had never been a part of Poland, but after 1945 was "administered" by Poland. As I stated in 1980, the "Poland" mark is post World War II. It was not in use between 1916 and 1918; those dates have been historically attributed to that particular mark incorrectly. The source of this misinformation is not known, but those years or the 1919 – 1921 period shown by German reference books on ceramic marks is wrong. According to talks with Herr Soppa by Ron Capers in 1991, the R.S. Poland mark may have been implemented in order to recapture some of the American market.

The exact length of time that the "R.S. Poland" mark was in use is not known, but it probably was not for too many years. Soppa states that it really would not have been possible for much, if any, new porcelain to have been made in Tillowitz after 1945. The clay needed for its manufacture, kaolin, had always been imported from Czechoslovakia. After the war, that country was not interested in exporting this material because it was needed for the Czechoslovakian china industry. Moreover, the "Council for Mutual Economic Assistance," which was a type of economic union of member countries of the Warsaw Pact, was established in 1949. The council allowed Poland to make only ceramic wares, not true porcelain; porcelain production was allotted to East Germany and Czechoslovakia. After 1949, china manufactured by the former Schlegelmilch factory in Tillowitz was a type of stoneware, called "Porzellit." Thus, it is conceivable that the R.S. Poland mark was used only during the interval, about 1947 to 1949.

Chros'cicki (1974: 76) shows a new mark instituted by the factory about 1956. The new mark takes into account the fact that Tillowitz was not at that time in an area administered by the Polish government. It had become a *de facto* part of Poland as a consequence of political settlements at the end of World War II. The new mark bears a definite similarity to the RSP and RSG wreath marks as described in my first edition. A wreath with the initials "P" and "T" are printed above the words "Tulowice, Made in Poland." A photograph of that mark was not available for my 1980 edition, but the mark is shown in the Fourth Series, thanks to the efforts of Capers and the McCaslins. The Poland factory is currently in operation. A portion of the plant burned in 1970, but it was rebuilt (Wenke, 1984: 2).

Marks and photographs for the R.S. Company in Tillowitz other than the R.S. Prussia marks are included in the Fourth Series.

Chapter 2

R.S. Prussia Decoration

Decoration Methods

The decoration on R. S. Prussia is perhaps the most distinguishing characteristic of the china. To better understand how R. S. Prussia was decorated, a few comments should be made about porcelain decorating in general. After the porcelain paste is molded, it is fired to a state of translucency. Objects can then be decorated before they are fired a second time (to a state of vitreosity). If the decoration is applied before the second firing, it is permanent or sealed and cannot be damaged (except through breakage, of course). This type of decoration is called *under glaze decoration*. If however, the decoration is applied after the second firing, so called *over glaze decoration*, the decor can be scratched or damaged, especially through time, although vitreous-type paints may have been used. Whether the decoration was applied over or under the glaze can be determined by feeling. If the design or pattern cannot be differentiated from the undecorated parts of an object, the decoration is under the glaze. The pieces will have a glass-like feel all over. If, however, the decoration has a texture, usually grainy, it has been decorated over the glaze. Check the undecorated portion of an object, such as the bottom of a bowl or the inside of a vase, tankard or tea pot. These parts should have the glass-like feel, and when compared to the decorated parts, the difference in texture will be more obvious. (Note that the bases of some items such as trays and vases are unglazed, not vitreous, in order to give the objects more surface grippage.)

Porcelain is decorated, under or over the glaze, by one of three methods: *handpainting, transfer designs* or a *combination of handpainting and transfer designs*. Handpainting is the most costly method because of the time it takes, plus it requires a skilled artist. All porcelain was handpainted during the earliest years of the industry. Toward the latter part of the 1800s, however, most porcelain manufacturers were taking advantage of the transfer method. Transfer decorating is a process where a particular design is made on paper, stone, or plates (lithography) and transferred to another object. The original design, like the mold, can be used over and over again on many types of objects. This process was developed first in England and was used on English earthenwares before it was used on porcelain. Transfer decoration is cheaper than handpainted designs. It also allows many objects to have identical decoration. Transfer decorating, just as using the same mold, is one of the main reasons for the rapid growth of the European porcelain exporting business. The process itself, though, is not really so simple as it may sound. Designs can be made, but they must be colored. The coloring process, if the decoration is to have more than one color, must go through several stages before the transfer is ready to use. Early transfer designs were hand colored; later ones were "printed."

Whether an object has been handpainted or decorated by transfer can be determined by examining it with a loupe or magnifying glass. If a uniform series of dots or lines can be seen, the piece has been decorated by transfer. If brush stokes or irregular lines are seen, the object was handpainted. It was a common practice for porcelain manufacturers to combine these methods during the late 1800s, especially as gold frequently was used lavishly as part of the decoration. A main design was applied by transfer, but embellishments could be added by hand. Also enameling, thickly applying paint in small areas creating a raised or relief appearance, was often used, particularly on floral designs.

Most RSP-marked porcelain was decorated by transfer design or a combination of transfer designs and hand applied gold or enameling. The decoration was over the glaze. This accounts for the wear on some of the designs. Although some pieces were handpainted, very few were, compared to those decorated by transfer. If pieces were handpainted at the factory, the word "Handpainted" is a part of the back mark (see Mark 6). Also some items marked "Handpainted" may refer only to enameling or trim with the major design actually a transfer.

Not all porcelain was decorated at the factory, of course, and undecorated pieces are referred to as blanks. Many blanks manufactured by European porcelain companies were exported to this country during the late 1800s. These pieces were decorated by amateurs or professionals for their own use or to be sold. China painting was considered quite an accomplished art form at that time. Blanks with German, French, or Japanese marks which have been decorated by Americans from this era are quite common. RSP-marked blanks, however, are quite rare, but they do exist. The examples I have personally seen had the RSP green mark with the mark of a decorating company. From some other double markings on RSP, it seems that perhaps some RSP blanks may also have been decorated by European or German decorators of the period.

Decoration Themes

The world of art encompasses many subjects and symbols. RSP porcelain was decorated with examples of popular subjects and artistic symbols. The decoration themes of RSP porcelain can be categorized as animal, bird, figural, floral, portrait, and scenic. In many instances pieces are decorated with more than one theme. That mixture of themes is only one of the many decorative characteristics that makes RSP so appealing to collectors.

Floral themes are the most common, while animal and fruit themes are the most scarce. Several of the portrait and figural themes were transfer decorations based on the original works of famous artists of the eighteenth and nineteenth centuries. At that time in history, the late 1800s, many porcelain manufacturers used such transfers on their products. The transfers are not precise replicas of the original paintings, although many of them have the artist's name or initials included in the picture as a signature. Such a signature implies that the artist actually painted that print and signed it. In the first place an exact print, made from the artist's original painting, would have the artist's signature if it appeared on the original painting. But the transfers were not made from the original paintings. The transfers were copied by other artists and print makers. They included the signature or initials probably to indicate who had in fact been responsible for the original painting. One of the most common ideas or mis-stated interpretations concerning RSP decoration is that such pieces are artist signed. RSP porcelain which has a famous artist's name as part of the decoration was not decorated by that artist, nor the transfer made by that artist. Knowledge of the years when those particular artists lived would quickly show that idea to be incorrect. Most of them had died before RSP items were manufactured. The "signed" name, however, does cause confusion. Pieces are often advertised for sale, for example, which say, "such and such a plate, signed Lebrun." This makes it look as though Lebrun painted the plate and signed it. Experienced collectors of course are aware that this is not so. They know the pieces are not handpainted or that the transfers were not made by the artist. But new collectors may not be aware of this and may be misled.

Background Colors

Another distinguishing characteristic of RSP is the background colors. These colors are not the "finish" on an object but are part of the decorative themes. The usual subject of decoration was not left unadorned. A portrait or scenic transfer, for example, was not simply placed on the white vitreous glaze of the object and considered finished. Background colors were necessary to highlight the central theme. These colors were applied over the glaze by transfer methods just like the decoration transfers. The background colors are not to be confused with glazes which are a type of finish. Both background colors and glazes, of course, can be used to decorate an object. The surreal floral and leaf images are a part of the background colors.

Interesting features of the background colors are the many different shades of a particular color or combination of colors which were used. Primarily in brown, blue, green, or yellow, these background colors varied from very dark to very light shades. Other colors such as red, pink, lavender, and orange were treated in the same way although these are not so prevalent. The colors often have a mottled appearance on some pieces. Colors were also combined: the backgrounds are not all necessarily shades of just one color. Some specific subjects are associated with certain background colors. The Mill and Castle scenes, for example, are usually in brown or blue-green tones. This unique characteristic of background colors really defies proper word description. It is best understood and appreciated by viewing the photographs.

Finishes

One of the most important characteristics of RSP products is the finish decoration. Finish is defined as a particular surface quality of an object. After a piece of porcelain is decorated (or sometimes before) with a specific subject and background, another type of glaze (a vitreous or glassy coating) can be applied. There are many different types and colors of glazes which result from specific materials used to achieve the desired effect. The glazes can be applied over all the surface of an object or just on certain parts of the surface. For example, a portrait item might have an iridescent glaze surrounding it, but the portrait itself would not have this glaze. Sometimes only the border or small parts of the border have a different or additional finish from the rest of the body of the piece. Some of the glazes or finishes on RSP porcelain include the following:

Glossy: a shiny finish with a slick look (either high gloss, very shiny or lacquered in appearance, or semi-gloss with only a light sheen);

Iridescent: glazes which have different colors that appear to change with varying amounts of light;

Lustre: a metallic glaze which has a shiny, iridescent effect;

Matte: a dull finish, not lustrous or shiny;

Pearl: a shiny finish, usually white, and not iridescent;

Pearl Button: a hard pearl finish which resembles a pearl button;

Pearlized: an iridescent, lustre type finish;

Satin: a semi-matte glaze, usually white, resembling satin in look and texture;

Solid Colors: metallic glazes composed of only one color such as red, green, or cobalt blue;

Tiffany: a brown, green, or bronze iridescent glaze which resembles Tiffany art glass;

Watered Silk: a smudged color effect, usually on satin finishes, which resembles a water spot on silk or satin.

In addition to the different types of glazes used on RSP, gold was an important finishing touch on many pieces. Objects were gilded on the borders (lightly or heavily), on bases, handles, and feet, or on outlines of designs formed in the mold. A brief look at the photographs immediately shows how much gold was actually a part of the decor of so many items. One specific type of gold decoration is referred to as the Tapestry finish. Parts of an object, borders or medallions, rarely the entire surface, have small bead forms painted gold all over the circumscribed area. Stippling is the term used to describe this form of beading. Stippled designs were occasionally painted or glazed with colors other than gold.

Objects may also have gold stencilled designs: repetitive patterns made in stencil form and painted gold. These designs are usually applied as outer or inner border enhancement. Another use of gold was in spray or mottled form over the surface or on certain parts of the surface. Gold was an important part of the decorating process for most nineteenth century porcelain manufacturers. This is understandable for gold imparts such a rich look. Porcelain produced during the latter part of the first quarter of the twentieth century, however, was not lavishly decorated with gold. Silver trims on porcelain came into style during this period. Silver trim was less expensive and less attractive than gold finishes.

RSP porcelain objects present such a beautiful over-all effect that it is perhaps easy to look at a piece without really seeing it. If you take the time to examine a piece thoroughly, from the intricate mold designs and translucency to the decorative subjects, colorful background, unique finishes, and gold embellishments, you will have an even greater appreciation for this beautiful porcelain.

Chapter 3

R.S. Prussia
Marks

Red Star and Wreath Marks

The R. S. Prussia mark is distinctive, incorporating a wreath and star with the initials "R. S." and "Prussia." This mark was used by the Reinhold Schlegelmilch china factories in both the cities of Suhl and Tillowitz. While both factories may have used the R. S. Prussia mark during some of the time period after 1894 when the Tillowitz factory was established and before the Suhl factory closed in 1917, it is most likely that the RSP mark was used in Tillowitz after 1917 for just a few years. Marks 4, 5, and 6 definitely show the RSP mark in use at Tillowitz, because the additional Tillowitz mark was added to the RSP mark. The relatively few examples found with both the RSP mark and the Tillowitz mark are further indication that such marks were not used for any long period of time.

The beginning date for the R. S. Prussia mark was discussed in all of my books. In the Third Series, I presented a chart showing different dates for the mark according to several reference sources. The years of 1904 or 1905 are given as the first date the mark was registered (Röntgen, 1981; Danckert, 1984.) I noted earlier, however, that the first time a mark is registered does not necessarily mean that is the first year pieces appeared with that mark. To date, however, no records have surfaced to indicate the precise year when the red wreath and star mark was first used at the Reinhold Schlegelmilch factory. I have maintained that the mark was probably begun in the late 1800s, and this may well be the case. I think, at this point, however, that the date of the early 1900s until 1920 might be a more precise time period for denoting when the mark was used.

Pieces shown in the photographs are marked with one of the R. S. Prussia marks shown here, and thus there is no reference to a particular mark number in the captions of the pictures. Some unmarked items have been included as well, and that notation is made in the caption of the photograph.

Mark 1. *Red, Suhl.*

Mark 2. *Green, Suhl.*

Mark 3. *Red, with gold "Handpainted."*

Mark 4. *Green RSP with red script RSG, Tillowitz.*

Mark 5. *Red RSP with red script RSG, Tillowitz.*

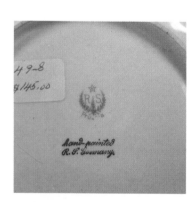

Mark 6. *Red RSP with gold RSG and "hand-painted," Tillowitz.*

Chapter 4

Popular Figural, Portrait, Scenic, and Bird Decorations

The Melon Eaters and Dice Throwers

(Plates 1-23)

The Melon Eaters or Melon Boys are perhaps the most popular figural decorations on R. S. Prussia china. These scenes were based on paintings by Bartolomé Esteban Murillo, a Spanish artist (1618 – 1682). A series of beggar children paintings including "Boys Eating Melon," and "Boys Throwing Dice," are some of his most popular works.

On RSP items, the Melon Boys portray two small boys in tattered clothing with one holding a piece of melon above his mouth and the other child looking at him. A dog and a basket of fruit are in the foreground. The Dice Throwers scene is composed of three boys. Two are kneeling at a game of dice played on a stone, and the third child is standing in the background, eating a piece of fruit. A dog is at his side.

Pieces of R. S. Prussia which are decorated with these themes do not always have all the scene on each piece. Sometimes only one of the Melon Boys is shown, or sometimes the third child in the Dice Throwers appears alone. Often on chocolate pots or vases, the full scene will be on the front of the piece, and then only a single figure on the reverse side. Pieces decorated with the boys from both transfers can also be found. A few examples shown here incorporate both subjects on a single item. Thus it is clear that the porcelain decorators saw these two transfers as related just as they did many of the other decoration subjects. The mix or pairing of two or more subjects usually enhances the value. Of the two subjects, the Melon Eaters seem to have been used on R. S. Prussia somewhat more than the Dice Throwers. Thus, values are a little higher for the latter, depending on object, mold, and finishes.

The "Melon Boys" and "Dice Throwers" are found on many of the same molds. Usually they are on some of the most elaborate molds such as Molds 18, 645, and 963 (the Ribbon and Jewel Molds) or a number of other "jeweled" molds found in Vases and Urns. Simple molds such as Mold 300 (Rope Edge) decorated with either of the figures are lower in value than the jeweled or fancy molds with the same decor. Brown or green tone backgrounds with little gold as well as the simple shape account for the lower prices. Cobalt blue or deep rose finishes, extensive gold work, and unique shapes add considerably to the value of pieces. Note, too, that the number of "jewels" decorated as opals also raises the dollar amount of the piece.

Mold 82 and its companion Mold 643 (the Point and Clover molds) are also jeweled molds which were decorated with the Melon Boys and Dice Throwers. Sometimes, however, depending on the finish, the jewels are not decorated, and thus a less rich appearance is the result. Prices are usually lower for such pieces. An exception is the cider pitcher shown on the facing page. The value is quite high because this particular piece of china decorated with the Melon Eaters is considered more rare than other pieces such as bowls and plates with the same decoration.

In the following photographs, examples with the Melon Boys, whole scene or single boy, are shown first. The Dice Throwers, whole scene or single boy, follow. A few pieces with both subjects are at the end of this section.

Plate 1. Bowl, 9"d, Mold 18, Ribbon and Jewel Mold, Melon Eaters; gold stipple and stencilled work frame the figures with opalescent jewels and heavy gold "ribbon" highlighting the border. $1,400.00 – 1,600.00.

Plate 2. Bowl, 10½"d, Mold 82, Point and Clover Mold, Melon Eaters; lavender-brown background with shadow flowers; undecorated jewels. $1,200.00 – 1,400.00.

Plate 3. Cider Pitcher, 6"h, 6"w, Mold 643, companion to Mold 82, Melon Eaters; lavender-brown background; undecorated jewels. $3,000.00 – 3,500.00.

Plate 4. Celery Dish, 13½"l, 7"w, pierced handles, Mold 300, Melon Eaters; lavender-brown background. $550.00 – 650.00.

Plate 5. Vase, 13½"h, Mold 901, Melon Eaters; red highlights with gold trim; single Melon Eater on reverse (not shown). $2,000.00 – 2,200.00.

Plate 6. Vase, 4½"h, salesman's sample, Mold 909, single figure from the Melon Eaters; iridescent Tiffany finish on top and base overlaid with gold stencilled designs. $400.00 – 600.00.

Plate 8. *Vase, 9"h, Mold 941, open work at base, Melon Eaters decorate center panel of vase on a shaded green background with light cream side panels; heavy gold trim with 16 opalescent jewels. $2,800.00 – 3,000.00.*

Plate 7. *Vase, 9¼"h, Mold 932, Melon Eaters; iridescent lavender finish with red highlights and opalescent jewels. $3,000.00 – 3,400.00.*

Plate 9. *Vase, 11"h, Mold 952, Pillow Mold, Melon Eaters; lavender-brown background with shadow flowers; 32 opalescent jewels, gold trim. $3,600.00 – 4,000.00.*

Plate 10. Plate, 8½"d, Mold 18, Dice Throwers; gold stippled work with opalescent jewels highlighting gold ribbon around border. $1,600.00 – 1,800.00.

Plate 12. Demitasse Sugar, 3"h, and Creamer 2½"h, Mold 643, companion to Mold 82; single figure from the Dice Throwers on each piece. $1,000.00 – 1,200.00 set.

Plate 11. Oval Bowl, 13"l, pierced handles, Mold 82, Point and Clover Mold, Dice Throwers; lavender-brown background, gold accents. $1,400.00 – 1,600.00.

Plate 13. Tea Set, Mold 643, Teapot decorated with the Dice Throwers; Creamer and Sugar decorated with the single figure from the group; cobalt blue finish at top and base, undecorated jewels, gold trim. $2,800.00 – 3,200.00 set.

Plate 14. Bowl, 10¼"d, Mold 97, Dice Throwers decorate center with the single Melon Boy shown in the four medallions around the border; heavy gold work, unmarked. $2,000.00 – 2,200.00.

Plate 15. Plate, 8½"d, Mold 300, Dice Throwers; lavender-brown background with shadow flowers and gold stencilled designs around inner border. $800.00 – 1,000.00.

Plate 16. Vase, 6"h, Mold 907, Dice Throwers, unmarked. $450.00 – 550.00.

Plate 17. Vase, 7"h, Mold 951, Pillow Mold, Dice Throwers; shaded green background; two opals on each side, gold trim, unmarked. $2,500.00 – 3,000.00.

Plate 18. Covered Urn, 12"h, Mold 964, Dice Throwers; shaded blue to green background, 14 opalescent jewels, gold trim. $3,000.00 – 3,500.00.

Plate 20. *Sugar and Creamer Set, Mold 645, companion to Ribbon and Jewel Molds, the single figure from the Dice Throwers decorates sugar and the single figure from the Melon Boys decorates creamer. $1,400.00 – 1,600.00.*

Plate 19. *Covered Urn, 9¼"h, Mold 963, companion to Molds 18 and 645 (Ribbon and Jewel Molds), single Boy from the Dice Throwers; cream background, gold work, and opalescent jewels. $2,500.00 – 3,000.00.*

Plate 21. *Chocolate Set, Mold 645 decorated with the Melon Eaters on the Chocolate Pot and single figures from the Melon Eaters and Dice Throwers on the cups. Chocolate Pot, $3,500.00 – 4,000.00; Cup and Saucer Sets, $275.00 – 325.00.*

Plate 22. Demitasse Pot, 9¾"h, Mold 645, Boy from the Dice Throwers decorates one side and Boy from the Melon Eaters decorates the other side; opalescent jewels, gold beaded work, and gold trim on shaded cream background. $3,000.00 – 3,500.00.

Plate 23. Reverse of Demitasse Pot in preceding photograph with figure of the single Melon Eater.

The Four Seasons
(Plates 24-68)

Decorations denoting the seasonal changes of the year have been portrayed by artists throughout history. Certain symbols were used to identify each of the four seasons. Spring was often symbolized by a young woman holding flowers or wearing flowers in her hair. Spring was also represented by a young man and young woman with flowers or birds in the scene. Summer might be portrayed by a woman holding corn or fruit, or by reapers in the field. Grapes and vine leaves were associated with Autumn. Winter reflected protection against the cold. This season was sometimes presented as an old man by the fire, or by people ice skating. Snow, of course, was usually a part of the picture.

It is not surprising that the "Four Seasons" transfers on R. S. Prussia china exemplify some of the same characteristics as other contemporary renditions of the theme. Beautiful women, elegantly but scantily gowned, are shown with specific symbols to represent their seasons. Spring wears flowers in her hair and holds a flowering dogwood branch in her arms. Winter's arms are clasped in front of her as a shield against the cold. Trees are covered with an imagery of snow, and snowflakes and a holly branch complete the scene. Summer holds red poppies near her head, and a wheat field serves as the background. Autumn wears a yellow-peach rose at the top of her gown. The wind appears to be blowing her hair and scarf as well as the leaves swirling around her.

The Seasons are usually found on some of the most popular floral molds such as Molds 9 and 609 (Fleur-de-lis); 25 and 628 (Iris); and 28, 519, and 526 (Carnation). Vases in the Art Nouveau molds like Molds 900, 916, 948, and 953, often are decorated with one of the Four Seasons. These particular molds indicate that the transfers were used during the early 1900s prior to World War II. While it is not uncommon to find examples of china made by other factories with the same figural or portrait transfers found on R. S. Prussia, it is rarely the case with the Four Seasons. But as with other transfers, the Reinhold Schlegelmilch factory was not the exclusive user of these particular renditions of the Seasons.

On R. S. Prussia china, one season is usually the central theme, but sometimes all four seasons appear together, in cameo or medallion form. Occasionally, one of the Seasons is combined with some other transfer, such as the Cottage scene. All four Seasons on one piece is very desirable among collectors. Examples are found on fancy molds such as 88, 95, and 102 as shown on pages 35 and 36. Bowls, plates, and trays seem to have been made as specific sets of the seasons. Collectors are anxious to acquire a matching set. Chocolate, tea, and coffee services appear to have been decorated with the same season on all pieces. Mixed sets, however, are probably easier to assemble.

Regarding value, top prices are paid for examples decorated with all of the Four Seasons. Pieces with one of the Seasons and another scene such as the Cottage or Mill are also valued highly. Two scenes, however, are not as valuable as three scenes. Tankards and Chocolate or Demitasse Pots and Sets decorated with one of the Seasons are favorite items among collectors, and thus values are among the highest for prime pieces. While vases are often the same size as tankards or chocolate pots, they realize lower dollar amounts. Cobalt, red, or Tiffany finishes combined with heavy gold trim and gold tapestry work greatly enhance the value of any Season-decorated china. Lack of gold and matte or pearl luster finishes with the Seasons usually lowers the value.

The photographs of the Four Seasons are shown first with an example of each Season in a set of four plates. These are followed by several examples with all four figures on one piece. The remainder of the pictures are divided into separate sections of each individual Season decorating a variety of molds and objects.

Plate 24. Plate, 9"d, Mold 343, Winter; heavy gold tapestry finish overlaid with clusters of pink roses decorates this and the following three plates. Note the deep red glaze on the inner border of the Spring and Autumn portraits which increases their value. Each portrait in this set is also distinguished by what collectors refer to as a "keyhole frame." $1,800.00 – 2,000.00.

Plate 25. Plate, 9"d, Mold 343, Spring. $2,000.00 – 2,200.00.

Plate 26. *Plate, 9"d, Mold 343, Summer. $1,800.00 – 2,000.00.*

Plate 27. *Plate, 9"d, Mold 343, Autumn. $2,000.00 – 2,200.00.*

Plate 28. *Bowl, 10¾"d, Mold 88; portrait medallions of each of the Four Seasons encircle the inner border. Note that Summer was used twice in this decoration. Pink and white roses, FD3, decorate the center of the bowl, framed by gold stencilled designs. $2,400.00 – 2,800.00.*

Plate 29. *Bowl, 10½"d, Mold 95, a very ornate mold with fancy scroll work; a double portrait of Autumn and Winter decorates the deep inner borders of two sides of the bowl; multi-colored poppies, FD 16, are the center design. "Germany" printed in gold accompanies the R. S. Prussia mark on this piece. $3,200.00 – 3,600.00.*

Plate 30. *Bowl, 10½"d, Mold 102; all four Seasons are portrayed with a portrait of a different Season shown at the top of one petal of a molded floral design in the center of the bowl; raised gold outlines the petal shape, and gold stencilled work is featured on the center interior. $4,000.00 – 5,000.00.*

Plate 31. *Plate, 8½"d, Mold 23, Stippled Floral Mold, Winter portrait; light blue-green background with a narrow band of gold forming inner border. $1,000.00 – 1,200.00.*

Plate 32. *Relish Dish, 9½"l, 4½"w, Mold 25, Iris Mold, Winter portrait; satin finish with gold trim. $1,200.00 – 1,400.00.*

Plate 33. *Bowl, 10"d, Mold 25, Winter portrait framed by a molded recessed floral design; satin finish on light lavender background. $2,000.00 – 2,200.00.*

Plate 34. *Covered Sugar, 5"h, and Creamer, 3"h, Mold 456. Winter portrait. $1,200.00 – 1,400.00 set.*

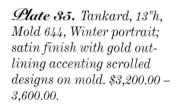

Plate 35. *Tankard, 13"h, Mold 644, Winter portrait; satin finish with gold outlining accenting scrolled designs on mold. $3,200.00 – 3,600.00.*

Plate 36. *Coffee Pot, 8"h, Mold 664, Winter portrait outlined by a gold beaded frame; cobalt blue finish on center body framing figure; heavy gold work overlaid with small pink flowers; the spout is undecorated, but the Art Nouveau shaped handle is heavily gilded. $3,400.00 – 3,800.00.*

Plate 37. *Vase, 10"h, Mold 900, Winter portrait on iridescent rose finish; gold beaded frame and gold finish on handles and base. $1,800.00 – 2,000.00.*

Plate 38. *Vase, 10¼"h, Mold 916, Grape Mold, Winter portrait; embossed grapes and leaves at top and base are painted gold. $1,600.00 – 1,800.00.*

Plate 39. *Vase, 9"h, Mold 925, Winter portrait; iridescent lavender Tiffany finish overlaid with gold stencilled designs. $1,500.00 – 1,700.00.*

Plate 40. *Vase, 9"h, Mold 929, Fleur-de-lis Mold, Winter portrait; lavender iridescent finish with embossed mold designs painted gold. $1,500.00 – 1,700.00.*

Plate 41. *Vase, 9"h, Mold 946, Winter portrait on dark blue-green background; gold trim. $1,400.00 – 1,600.00.*

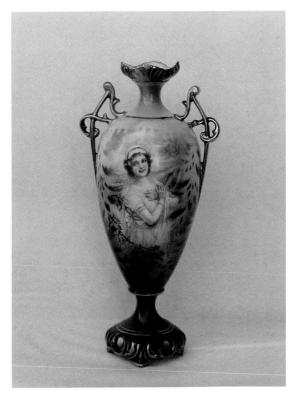

Plate 42. Vase, 8"h, Mold 948, Winter portrait; shaded blue-green background; gold handles and trim. $1,400.00 – 1,600.00.

Plate 43. Vase, 8"h, Mold 954, Winter portrait; iridescent rose finish; gold beaded frame and gold handles. $1,800.00 – 2,000.00.

Plate 44. *Relish Dish, 9¾"l, 4¼"w, Mold 25, Iris Mold, Spring portrait, satin finish. $1,200.00 – 1,400.00.*

Plate 45. *Demitasse Pot, 9¼"h, Mold 628, companion to Iris Mold 25, Spring portrait; gold outlining at base of spout and on floral designs of mold. $3,000.00 – 3,500.00.*

Plate 46. *Tray, pierced handles, Mold 28, Carnation Mold, Spring portrait. The placement of the Season in a vertical rather than horizontal position seems to indicate that the tray was designed to display rather than to set on a dresser! $2,000.00 – 2,200.00.*

Plate 47. *Bowl, 10½"d, Mold 78, Spring portrait; deep rose finish accented with gold surrounds dome shapes around border; pink poppies, FD7, decorate the dome shapes. $2,200.00 – 2,400.00.*

Plate 48. *Demitasse Pot, 9½"h, Mold 644, Spring portrait; iridescent Tiffany finish with heavy gold work frames the figure; "Gesetzlich Geschutzt" (patent mark) printed in gold with the R. S. Prussia mark. $3,500.00 – 3,800.00.*

Plate 49. *Vase, 10¼"h, Mold 924, Spring portrait outlined with a gold beaded frame; pearl luster finish on body with a green iridescent finish at base and neck; gold trim. $800.00 – 1,000.00.*

Plate 50. *Vase, 8½"h, Mold 953, Spring portrait; cobalt blue finish at top and base; neck, handles, and foot painted gold; unmarked. $2,200.00 – 2,400.00.*

Plate 51. *Cake Plate, 10½"d, Mold 9, "Fleur-de-lis" Mold, Summer portrait; dark shaded green background with the molded designs thinly outlined in gold. $1,600.00 – 1,800.00.*

Plate 52. *Tea Set: Pot, 6"h, Sugar, 5½"h, Creamer, 4"h, Mold 609, companion to Mold 9, Summer portrait on all three pieces; shaded lavender background with satin finish. $2,800.00 – 3,200.00 set.*

Plate 53. *Bowl, 10"d, Mold 25, Iris Mold, Summer portrait on green background, framed by molded floral design outlined with gold stencil work; Tiffany bronze finish on outer border and Iris; white satin finish on inner border. $2,000.00 – 2,200.00.*

Plate 54. Bowl, 9½"d, Mold 25, Summer portrait; shaded pink background with satin finish. $2,200.00 – 2,400.00.

Plate 55. Celery Dish, 12"l, 5¾"w, Mold 25; Summer portrait combined with the Mill scene; pink roses with a watered silk finish have also been added to the decor; molded iris and border thinly trimmed with gold. $2,000.00 – 2,200.00.

Plate 56. Tankard, 13"h, Mold 525, Stippled Floral Mold, Summer portrait combined with the Cottage scene; dark green background on bottom half of tankard with a light yellow "sky" above figure and cottage. $3,600.00 – 4,000.00.

Plate 58. Chocolate Pot, 10"h, Mold 526, Summer portrait; pink roses accent decor; gold trim and gold outlining on molded floral designs. $3,500.00 – 3,800.00.

Plate 57. Covered Sugar, 5½"h, and Creamer, 4"h, Mold 526, Carnation Mold, Summer portrait; shaded lavender background with satin finish. $1,400.00 – 1,600.00.

Plate 59. Cake Plate, 9¼"d, Mold 10c, Leaf variation
Mold, Autumn portrait; dark green background covers
surface of plate with gold outlining of leaf designs
around border. $2,300.00 – 2,500.00.

Plate 60. Bowl, 12"d, Mold 28, Carnation Mold,
Autumn portrait; light lavender finish highlights molded
floral shapes. $2,200.00 – 2,400.00.

Plate 61. *Tray, 12"d, 7½"w, Mold 28, Autumn portrait. $2,000.00 – 2,200.00.*

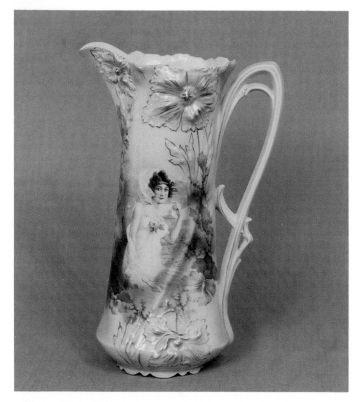

Plate 62. *Tankard, 13½"h, Mold 526, companion to Carnation Mold, Autumn portrait. $3,200.00 – 3,600.00.*

Plate 63. Cake Plate, 10¼"d, pierced handles, Mold 29, Lily Mold, Autumn portrait. $2,200.00 – 2,400.00.

Plate 64. Bowl, 10½"d, Mold 55, Autumn portrait; dark green background surrounds figure and outer edge of bowl with white floral shapes and inner border accented with gold. $2,000.00 – 2,200.00.

Plate 65. *Tray, 12"l, 7½"w, Mold 78, Autumn portrait outlined in gold. $1,400.00 – 1,600.00.*

Plate 66. *Cracker Jar, 7"h, Mold 628, Iris Mold, Autumn portrait; light lavender accents background and iris; gold trim. $2,400.00 – 2,600.00.*

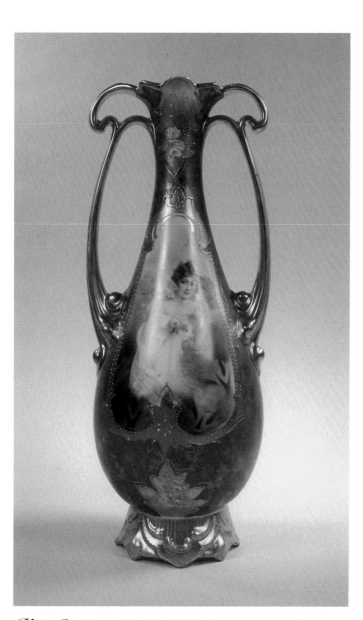

Plate 67. *Vase, 11"h, Mold 900, Autumn portrait; Tiffany bronze finish with gilded handles and base; gold stippled work on frame surrounding figure. $1,800.00 – 2,000.00.*

𝒫𝓁𝒶𝓉ℯ 68. *Ewer, 6½"h, Mold 900, Autumn portrait; cobalt blue finish at top and base heavily outlined in gold. $1,000.00 – 1,200.00.*

Portraits

Madame Lebrun, Countess Potocka, Madame Récamier
(Plates 69-103)

R. S. Prussia collectors are particularly partial to several decoration subjects which are generally referred to as portraits. Portrait transfers incorporate only the head and shoulders of a person and not the full figure as the Melon Eaters and Four Seasons do. The portraits most frequently found are Madame Lebrun in two different poses, Countess Potocka, and Madame Récamier.

Often, like the Four Seasons, all three of these portraits may have been used to decorate one piece of china. It is apparent that the factory decorators considered this group of women a "set." On molds, like the Medallion mold, however, four portraits rather than three were needed to decorate the medallion reserves. Both poses of Madame Lebrun solved this problem on some pieces. but it is not uncommon to find the same portrait used more than once on a piece.

The transfers were based on original portraits of these historical figures. Madame Lebrun (1755 – 1842) was not only a beautiful woman, but also she was a famous French artist. The decoration transfers of her portrait on R. S. Prussia are, in fact, based on her self portraits. Her full name was Marie Louise Elisabeth Vigeé. Her maiden name, Vigeé, is usually included in identifying her works. Madame Lebrun was a favorite artist of Queen Marie Antoinette. She painted many portraits of the Queen as well as portraits of other beautiful women of the era.

Two self portraits of Madame Lebrun are found on many different types of R. S. Prussia china. In one, she is wearing a white ribbon in her hair. The white draped neck of her gown can usually be seen. In the second portrait, she is wearing a white cap or bonnet and has a white ruche around her neck. Some versions of this portrait show more of her rust colored dress than others. I have used Lebrun I to identify the pose with the hair ribbon and Lebrun II for the other image with cap.

Madame Récamier (1777 – 1849) was another French beauty. Her full name was Jeanne Françoise Julie Adelaide Bernard. In 1793, she married a wealthy banker much older than she. After his eventual financial ruin, a marriage was arranged for her with Prince August of Prussia, but this never occurred. She was noted for her "salons," where she entertained important social and political figures of the time. The decoration transfer of her portrait was styled after the painting by Baron François Pascal Simon Gérard (1710 – 1837). He was born in Rome, but he is known as a French portrait painter. He painted for Napoleon, and he was court painter to the Bourbons after the Restoration. His painting of Madame Récamier in 1802 helped to spread his fame. He was made a baron by King Louis XVIII in 1819.

The third portrait, Countess Potocka, is portrayed with long red-brown curls enhanced by a blue ribbon. She is wearing a low-cut ruffled neck dress. This picture of the Countess accompanies an interesting account about her which was published in an 1873 New York publication, *The Aldine*. According to the article, Countess Potocka was born in 1773 and died in 1823. Her parents were Greek and lived in Constantinople. In 1786, her father sold her to a French ambassador, Marquis de Beauviere. This was the custom of the time, and due to her great beauty, a good price was obtained. Later, she was sold to a Russian general, Count Johann DeWitt. When he took her to the Court in St. Petersburg, she met Count Stanislaus Felix Potozki. He was so enamored with her that he bought her from the Russian general; thus she became a Countess. She was said to have spent the rest of her life on the Count's estate in the Crimea. (I thank Viola and Pete Zwern for furnishing me a copy of this article. The full story was printed in the October 1997 *Newsletter of the International Association of R. S. Prussia Collectors, Inc.*, pp. 20, 21.)

The portraits of these three women are found on a number of different R. S. Prussia molds. The transfers, however, are also found on china made by other European factories. Some of the most elaborate pieces are unmarked. These same portraits are also shown in my Fourth Series on Molds which are usually unmarked, such as Mold 29, the Lily Mold, or on pieces which are only marked "Royal Vienna." See that edition for elaboration on the subject. A few examples of china decorated with all three subjects are shown first. These are followed by pieces portraying each beauty individually.

Plate 69. Celery Dish, 14"l, 7"w, Mold 14, Medallion Mold; portraits clockwise of Potocka, Lebrun II, Récamier, and Lebrun I on medallions with gold tapestry finish on black border; Reflecting Poppies and Daisies, FD36, decorates the center. $1,200.00 – 1,400.00.

Plate 70. Cake Plate, 11"d, Mold 14; portrait medallions with very light gold tapestry work; portraits, clockwise of Potocka, Lebrun II, Lebrun I, Lebrun II, Récamier, and Lebrun I; pink and white floral garlands with miniature Hanging Baskets, FD44, decorate inner border; FD30a, a pink and a white rose with daisies surrounded by a garland, decorate the center; gold stencilled designs around the inner border; beaded rim painted gold. $1,000.00 – 1,200.00.

Plate 71. Plate or Charger, 12½"d, Mold 14; cameo portraits, clockwise, of Potocka, Récamier, Lebrun I, Récamier, and Lebrun I on dark cobalt blue border; the floral transfer has been placed off-center in the middle of the plate. Note that this floral decoration, FD12, is the same transfer as FD30a in Plate 70 except FD12 has a pink rose offshoot and FD30a incorporates the garland around the design; unmarked. $1,600.00 – 1,800.00.

Plate 72. Oval Handled Bowl, 11"l, Mold 14; portraits of Lebrun I and Récamier are at top of the piece with Potocka and Lebrun II at the bottom; a wide cobalt blue band outlined in gold forms the inner border; FD6, pink Poppies and Lily of the Valley, framed by gold stencilled designs decorates the center; a light green pearlized luster and gold trim highlight the outer border; unmarked. $1,400.00 – 1,600.00.

Plate 73. *Bowl, 9½"d, Mold 14a, Medallion variation Mold; Lebrun II in center of piece with, clockwise: Récamier, Lebrun I, Lebrun II, Potocka, and Lebrun I in the oval reserves on the border; each medallion is framed with gold and has a raised gold floral design on the left side; the cobalt blue inner border is overlaid with gold stencilled designs, and the outer border has a gold tapestry finish. $1,600.00 – 1,800.00.*

Plate 74. *Chocolate Set: Pot, 11"h, Cups, 3"h, Mold 517, Lily Mold; Lebrun II portrait encircled with a gold beaded frame on chocolate pot; light to dark rose finish on top and base; gold stencilled designs and gold trim. The cups are similarly decorated with portraits of Potocka and Récamier. $4,000.00 – 5,000.00 set.*

Plate 75. *Tea Set: Teapot, Sugar, and Creamer, Mold 517, Récamier portrait on Teapot and Sugar with Lebrun I portrait on creamer; Tiffany bronze finish. $2,200.00 – 2,500.00 set.*

Plate 76. *Coffee Set: Coffee Pot, 9½"h, Sugar, and Creamer; Mold 664, Récamier portrait decorates Coffee Pot with portrait of Lebrun I on Sugar and Creamer; green tinted background with rose highlights and gold trim; unmarked. $3,000.00 – 4,000.00 set.*

Plate 77. Footed Bowl, 10½"d, ten petal feet, Mold 29, Lily Mold, Lebrun I portrait; small blue enameled flowers on gold finish surround portrait; unmarked. $2,200.00 – 2,400.00.

Plate 78. Celery Dish, 12"l, 5½"d, pierced handles, Mold 29, Lebrun I portrait; gold Green Key border on Tiffany bronze finish; gold outer and inner borders with stippled work; unmarked. $1,400.00 – 1,600.00.

Plate 79. *Bowl, 10"d, Mold 29, Lebrun I portrait; Tiffany bronze finish; unmarked. $1,200.00 – 1,400.00.*

Plate 80. *Oval Bowl, 13"l, 8½"w, Mold 29, Lebrun I portrait with green iridescent Tiffany finish; unmarked. $1,400.00 – 1,600.00.*

Plate 82. *Coffee Pot, 9½"h, Mold 631, companion to Medallion Mold, Lebrun I cameo portrait on gold tapestry background; Reflecting Poppies and Daisies, FD36, on body; black finish on top and base. (Madame Récamier is the portrait on the reverse side, not shown.) $1,800.00 – 2,000.00.*

Plate 81. *Tankard, 15"h, Mold 517, companion to Lily Mold; Lebrun I portrait in gold stippled frame; rose finish; unmarked. $2,000.00 – 2,400.00.*

Plate 83. *Vase, 10"h, Mold 956, Lebrun I portrait; pearl luster finish on body with green finish at top and base; opalescent jewels at base; gold beaded frame surrounds portrait; fancy handles at top and base painted gold; unmarked. $1,200.00 – 1,400.00.*

Plate 84. *Relish Dish, 9½"l, 5"w, Mold 18, Ribbon and Jewel Mold. Lebrun II portrait framed by gold beading in center of piece; Tiffany bronze finish on ribbon part of mold with opalescent jewels. $400.00 – 500.00.*

Plate 85. *Sugar, 5½"h, Creamer, 4"h, Mold 645, companion to Mold 18, Ribbon and Jewel Mold, Lebrun II portrait on gold tapestry reserve; Tiffany bronze finish on ribbon part of mold with opalescent jewels. $1,400.00 – 1,600.00 set.*

Plate 86. *Bowl, 9¾"d, Mold 23, Stippled Floral Mold, Lebrun II portrait; light to dark blue inner border; unmarked. $800.00 – 1,000.00.*

Plate 87. *Relish Dish, 9¾"l, 4¼"w, Mold 29, Lily Mold with handle variation, Lebrun II portrait; gold finish on outer border; unmarked. $600.00 – 800.00.*

Plate 88. *Coffee Pot, 10½"h, Mold 517, companion to Mold 29, Lily Mold, Lebrun II portrait with green Tiffany finish at top and base; white handle and spout enhanced with gold outlining; unmarked. $1,800.00 – 2,000.00.*

Plate 89. *Sugar and Creamer, 5"h, Mold 517, Lebrun II portrait in gold beaded framework; rose finish. $1,200.00 – 1,400.00 set.*

Plate 90. *Bowl, 10"d, Mold 87, Lebrun II portrait; iridescent Tiffany finish on dome shapes of mold; undecorated parts of bowl are highlighted with gold outlining and beading. $1,200.00 – 1,400.00.*

Plate 91. *Chocolate Pot, 9½"h, Mold 572, companion to Mold 87, Lebrun II portrait with green Tiffany finish at top and base; gold stencilled designs and gold outlining accent undecorated parts of mold. $1,800.00 – 2,000.00.*

Plate 92. *Vase, 11½"h, Mold 960, Lebrun II portrait; cobalt blue finish at top extending around portrait and at base; gold enameled cross-hatch design on cream body; gilded handles; unmarked. $1,300.00 – 1,500.00.*

Plate 93. *Bowl, 10½"d, Mold 29, Potocka portrait; light rose shading on dome shapes; gold outlining; unmarked. $1,100.00 – 1,300.00.*

Plate 94. *Cake Plate, 9½"d, Mold 29, Potocka portrait; gold floral designs on white background around outer border; unmarked. $1,400.00 – 1,600.00.*

Plate 95. *Vase, 6"h, Mold 907, Potocka portrait in reserve on front; pearl luster finish; R. S. Prussia mark with Royal Vienna Mark. $400.00 – 500.00.*

Plate 96. *Potpourri Jar (pierced lid), 9"h, Mold 961, Potocka portrait; Lilac Clematis, FD39, on deep rose finish; gold handles and finial; rare object; unmarked. $1,400.00 – 1,600.00.*

Plate 97. *Bowl, 10"d, Mold 29, Récamier portrait; iridescent bronze Tiffany finish; gold stencilled inner border. $1,200.00 – 1,400.00.*

Plate 98. *Bowl, 7", Mold 30, companion to Lily Mold 29, Récamier portrait on background shading from light to dark green; gold outlining on lilies; unmarked. $700.00 – 900.00.*

Plate 99. *Bowl, 11"d, Mold 339, Récamier portrait; bronze iridescent Tiffany finish with floral designs on border tinted light pink and blue. $1,600.00 – 1,800.00.*

Plate 100. *Hairpin Box, 4½"l, 1½"h (molded hairpin is faintly visible in center of box), Mold 826, companion to Stippled Floral Mold 23; pink roses on a satin finish surround Récamier portrait; unmarked. $300.00 – 350.00.*

Plate 101. *Tankard, 13"h, Mold 525, companion to Stippled Floral Mold, Récamier portrait; yellow to green background overlaid with gold stencilled leaves; gold finish on top stippled part of mold; unmarked. $1,800.00 – 2,000.00.*

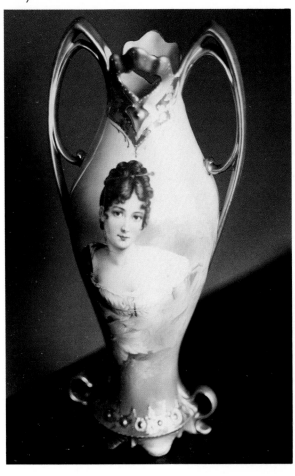

Plate 102. Vase, 13"h, Mold 956, Récamier portrait; FD39, Lilac Clematis, placed near base; deep rose finish accents top and base; gilded handles and foot; unmarked. $1,500.00 – 1,700.00.

Plate 103. Vase, 9¼"h, Mold 960, Récamier portrait; similar rose background with FD39 as in photo above; gold trim, unmarked. $1,200.00 – 1,400.00.

Scenic Decorations
Castle, Cottage, and Mill
(Plates 104-153)

Three scenic themes on R. S. Prussia china seem to have been designed to form complementary or matching sets. The Castle, Cottage, and Mill decorations usually have the same green or brown tone backgrounds. They are also found on the same molds. Mold 98 (Sawtooth) and Mold 632 (Ball Foot) seem to be the most popular for these scenes. From the large variety of different pieces with these transfers, it is easy to see that the R. S. factory thought that this particular type of decor would go over well with its customers. A number of vases with these decorations were featured in the 1906 Falker & Stern catalog.

The Castle or Church decoration could also be called the Village scene. It is difficult to determine if the dominant building in the picture is a church or a castle. Either would have been considered an appropriate subject at the time. This building has a tall spire with a cross on top, which usually indicates a church. There are several other buildings close to it which could indicate either an estate or a village. A man can be seen walking on a path toward the buildings, and a body of water is to his right. Collectors use the term Castle more frequently than any other, however, to refer to this scene.

The Cottage scene depicts a quaint house with a thatched roof. A small boy with a pack on his back can be seen going out the front door. Another figure, presumably the mother, is watching him from the window of the cottage.

The Mill theme is composed of a water mill and an adjoining cottage by a stream. The figure of a woman wearing an apron with a kerchief on her head are in the foreground. The water mill was a popular artist theme especially during the 1800s. A famous picture printer of the era was George Baxter (1804 – 1864). His print, titled "The Old Watermill" was based on a poem by Eliza Cook. The miller's house, the mill, and the miller's boy were the subjects of the poem. The transfer on R. S. Prussia china is not the same as Baxter's print, but it was probably the inspiration for it as the mill and adjoining cottage are quite similar.

The background colors for the Castle, Cottage, and Mill usually have a brown tone, shading from brown to light yellow to suggest ground and sky. A light lavender pearl luster finish is sometimes found with these background colors. Green backgrounds for these scenes are less common. There are actually two types of green finish. One is a dark, dull green tone while the other is sharper with a suggestion of turquoise.

The Castle, Cottage, and Mill decorations are so vivid and detailed that there are rarely other embellishments except gold trim. Heavily gilded pieces and cobalt blue finishes add greatly to the value of these decors. In general, the values for these scenes are less than for figural or portrait subjects, but are higher than floral decorations. It is rare to find one of the scenes combined with another unrelated decoration. When combinations are found, the second transfer determines the value. An example with the Mill and figure of Summer shown in Plate 55 is valued quite highly. The hatpin holder with the Mill combined with the Swallows in Plate 147 is in a much lower value range.

The first pictures are of a few items decorated with two or all of the three scenes. Individual examples of the Castle, Cottage, and Mill decorations follow. Background colors are not listed in the captions unless they are some color other than brown.

Plate 104. *Berry Set: Master Bowl, 10"d; Individual Bowls, 5½"d; Mold 98, Sawtooth Mold; all three scenes are found on this set with the Cottage scene on the serving bowl. Master Bowl, $600.00 – 800.00; Individual Bowls, $100.00 – 125.00 each.*

Plate 105. *Creamer, 3½"h, Mill scene; Sugar, 4"h, Cottage scene. Mold 576; turquoise green background at base. $400.00 – 600.00 set.*

Plate 106. Sugar and Creamer, 3½"h, Mold 644; Castle scene on Sugar and Mill scene on Creamer; turquoise green background. $450.00 – 650.00 set.

Plate 107. Cracker Jar, Mold 632, Ball Foot Mold; Castle scene on jar with Mill scene on lid. $400.00 – 600.00.

Plate 108. *Castle scene examples are shown on a number of molds and pieces in this and the following 16 pictures. Cake Plate, 12"d, Mold 9, Fleur-de-lis Mold. $600.00 – 700.00.*

Plate 109. *Center-piece Bowl, 12"d, Mold 90; heavy gilding around dome shapes and molded flowers. $800.00 – 1,000.00.*

Plate 110. *Oval Bowl, 13"l, 8"w, Mold 98, Sawtooth Mold. $800.00 – 1,000.00.*

Plate 111. *Celery Dish, 12¼"l, 6"w, Mold 98. $700.00 – 800.00.*

Plate 112. *Bowl, 10"d, Mold 181; pierced handle. $600.00 – 700.00.*

Plate 113. Plate, 8½"d, Mold 300, Rope Edge Mold; dark green background. $400.00 – 500.00.

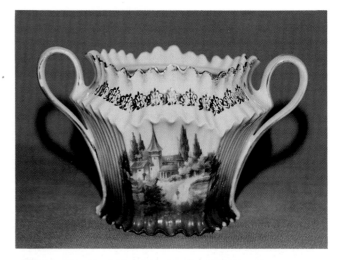

Plate 115. Sugar Bowl, 3½"h (without lid), Mold 568; turquoise green background. $300.00 – 350.00 (with lid).

Plate 114. Tankard, 13"h, Mold 525, Stippled Floral Mold. $1,500.00 – 1,700.00.

Plate 116. Jam Jar and Underplate, Mold 555.
$700.00 – 800.00.

Plate 117. Teapot, 5"h, Mold 576. $600.00 – 700.00.

Plate 118. Sugar, 4½"h, Creamer, 3"h, Mold 576. $450.00 – 650.00 set.

Plate 119. Sugar and Creamer, 4½"h, Mold 580.
$400.00 – 600.00 set.

Plate 120. Chocolate Pot, 9½"h, Mold 632, Ball Foot Mold. $1,000.00 – 1,200.00.

Plate 121. Teapot, 3½"h, Mold 632. $600.00 – 700.00.

Plate 122. Shaving Mug, 3½"h, Mold 644.
$300.00 – 400.00.

Plate 123. Cracker Jar, 5¾"h, Mold 644.
$600.00 – 700.00.

Plate 124. Vase, 7"h, Mold 923; the Royal Vienna
Mark as well as the R. S. Prussia mark is on this
piece. $800.00 – 1,000.00.

Plate 125. Cottage scene examples are shown in
this and the following nine pictures. Footed Bowl,
7½"d, four feet, Mold 90a. $500.00 – 600.00.

Plate 126. Tankard, 13"h, Mold 525, Stippled Floral Mold. $1,400.00 – 1,500.00.

Plate 127. Chocolate Set, Mold 632, Ball Foot Mold. Chocolate Pot, $1,000.00 – 1,200.00; Cup and Saucer, $150.00 – 200.00 each set.

Plate 128. *Cracker Jar, 7¼"h, Mold 643, Point and Clover Mold. $550.00 – 650.00.*

Plate 129. *Ewer, 8"h, Mold 901. $700.00 – 900.00.*

Plate 130. *Covered Urn, 12½"h, Mold 903. $1,800.00 – 2,000.00.*

Plate 131. Covered Urn, 11"h, Mold 903; cobalt blue finish at top and base overlaid with gold designs; handles and finial painted gold; unmarked. $2,500.00 – 2,700.00.

Plate 132. Vase, 5"h, Mold 909; dark green background. $275.00 – 350.00.

Plate 133. Vase, 7"h, Mold
951; dark green background.
$600.00 – 800.00.

Plate 134. Vase, 9"h,
Mold 932; jewels on neck
and body painted gold.
$600.00 – 800.00.

Plate 135. *Mill scene examples are shown in this and the following 18 pictures. Plate, 9½"d, Mold 25, Iris Mold; the Mill scene decorates the center, outlined with a gold floral design; FD7, two open bloom pink roses with two small buds, is in four locations around the inner border. The irises in the mold are tinted a delicate shade of pink; gold stencilled designs and gold outlining complete the decoration. $800.00 – 1,000.00.*

Plate 136. *Bowl, 10"d, Mold 90. $600.00 – 700.00.*

Plate 137. Plate, 8½"d, Mold 90; turquoise green background. $400.00 – 500.00.

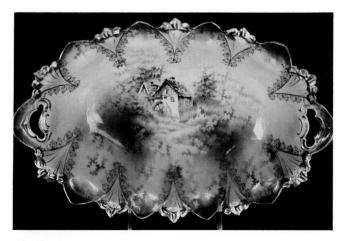

Plate 138. Oval Bowl, 13"l, 8"w, Mold 98, Sawtooth Mold. $800.00 – 1,000.00.

Plate 139. Bowl, 10"d, Mold 181, one handle. $650.00 – 750.00.

Plate 140. Relish Dish, 7"l, 4"w, Mold 300, Rope Edge Mold. $400.00 – 500.00.

Plate 141. Pitcher, Mold 522, companion to Ribbon and Jewel Mold. $800.00 – 1,000.00.

Plate 142. *Sugar Bowl, 4"h, Mold 535. $200.00 – 300.00.*

Plate 143. *Cracker Jar, 7"h, Mold 541; metal lid and handle. $700.00 – 800.00.*

Plate 144. *Sugar, 4"h, and Creamer, 3½"h, Mold 576. $400.00 – 600.00 set.*

Plate 145. Chocolate Set, Mold 632, Ball Foot Mold. Chocolate Pot, $1,000.00 – 1,200.00; Cup and Saucer, $150.00 – 200.00 each set.

Plate 146. Hatpin Holder, 4½"h, Mold 726. $350.00 – 450.00.

Plate 147. *Hatpin Holder, 4½"h, Mold 728; the Mill scene transfer and the Swallows or Bluebirds decorate this piece. $400.00 – 500.00.*

Plate 148. *Ferner, 3½"h, 8½"w, Mold 878; light lavender background on white body. $350.00 – 450.00.*

Plate 149. *Covered Urn, 11"h, Mold 903; cobalt blue finish at top and base with heavy gold accents. This urn is a companion to the one shown earlier with the Cottage scene; unmarked. $2,500.00 – 2,700.00.*

Plate 150. *Covered Urn, 12½"h, Mold 903. This urn is also a companion to another shown with the Cottage scene. $1,800.00 – 2,000.00.*

Plate 151. *Vase, 5½"h, Mold 909; Mill scene with Swallows. $450.00 – 650.00.*

Plate 152. *Vase, 4¼"h, salesman's sample, Mold 910; dark green background. $350.00 – 450.00.*

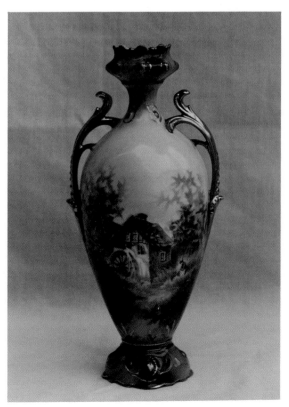

Plate 153. *Vase, 9½"h, Mold 942. $700.00 – 900.00.*

Old Man in the Mountain, Sheepherder 1, and Snowbird
(Plates 154 – 177)

The Old Man in the Mountain, Sheepherder, and Snowbird scenes are usually found as a single transfer on R. S. Prussia china. Sometimes, though, all three scenes can be found as a cameo on a single object made in Mold 14, the Medallion Mold, as illustrated in two pictures of this group. The pastel colors of all three scenes are complementary in the same way the brown and green tones are for the Castle, Cottage, and Mill scenes. Molds 7 and 14, Icicle and Medallion Molds, are often found with the Old Man in the Mountain and the Snowbird scenes.

Of these three transfers, the Old Man in the Mountain seems to have been used more than the other two scenes. Consequently, prices are usually higher for the Sheepherder and Snowbird decorated pieces. The Old Man in the Mountain presents a striking mountain and water decoration. The side view of the mountain in the foreground resembles the profile of a man's face. A sailboat on the lake completes the scene. Background colors suggest a cloudy sky. Some collectors refer to the Old Man in the Mountain scene as "Quiet Cove." Swans were often used as a second decoration with the Old Man in the Mountain, appearing with the scene or as a separate decoration on the other side of an object, like a pitcher or vase.

In my first book on R. S. Prussia, I gave numbers to two different versions of a Sheepherder scene. Sheepherder 2 is not frequently seen and may be found on examples with R. S. marks other than the R. S. Prussia mark. I have included it in the section on Scarce and Rare Decorations. The Sheepherder 1 scene, however, could also be considered scarce because few examples are seen.

Sheepherder 1 features a house in the country with a shepherd and his flock of sheep on a path in the foreground. This scene is highlighted by a large pink flowering tree and pink ground cover on either side of the path. A lake and mountains are in the background. Light green and light blue backgrounds are most common with this transfer, giving the appearance of a blue sky.

The Snowbird could, of course, be considered another bird decoration, but it is primarily a scenic view. A pair of Snowbirds is in the foreground of snow-covered land jutting into a lake. Evergreen trees, a barn type building, and mountains complete the view. The background colors reflect a sunset. Pieces may have a satin finish. Some examples have been seen with the snow scene without the Snowbirds.

Photographs of the Old Man in the Mountain scene are shown first. Examples with Sheepherder 1 and the Snowbird follow.

Plate 154. Bowl, 9½"d, Mold 14, Medallion Mold, Old Man in the Mountain center scene; cameo scenes of Sheepherder 1, Snowbird Scene (without the Snowbird), and Old Man in the Mountain on border medallions; black inner border overlaid with gold designs; wide gold outer border. $1,400.00 – 1,600.00.

Plate 155. *The Old Man in the Mountain scene is shown in this and the next 13 pictures. Bowl, 11"d, Mold 14, high glaze finish; Medallions are undecorated; gold trim; unmarked. $800.00 – 1,000.00.*

Plate 156. *Oval Bowl, 13"l, 8½"w, Mold 14. $900.00 – 1,100.00.*

Plate 157. *Lemonade Pitcher, 6½"h, Mold 631, companion to Medallion Mold but with a smooth base; Old Man in the Mountain decorates front with Swans (not shown) on reverse; black finish on base overlaid with gold stencilled designs. $1,000.00 – 1,200.00.*

Plate 158. *Celery Dish, 12"l, 6"w, Mold 7, Icicle Mold. $800.00 – 1,000.00.*

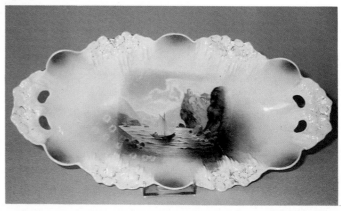

Plate 159. *Dessert Set (below): Cake Plate, 10"d with Individual Plates, 5"d; Mold 7, Icicle Mold. $1,300.00 – 1,500.00 set.*

Plate 161. *Bowl, 10½"d, Mold 266; satin finish.*
$900.00 – 1,100.00.

Plate 160. *Plate 8½"d, Mold 92, Popcorn Mold.*
$550.00 – 650.00.

Plate 162. *Bowl,*
11"d, Mold 304.
$800.00 – 1,000.00.

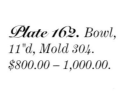

Plate 163. *Wall*
Plaque, 8½"d, Mold 426.
$700.00 – 800.00.

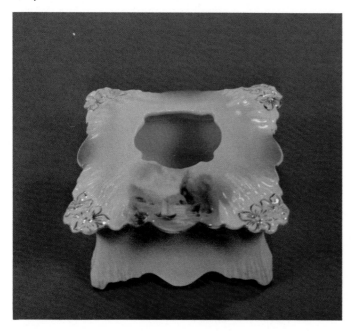

Plate 164. *Hair Receiver, 4"sq., Mold 806, companion to Icicle Mold; unmarked. $300.00 – 400.00.*

Plate 165. *Vase, 6½"h, Mold 908. $400.00 – 600.00.*

Plate 166. *Vase, 6½"h, Mold 915; Swans are shown with the Old Man in the Mountain on this piece. $500.00 – 700.00.*

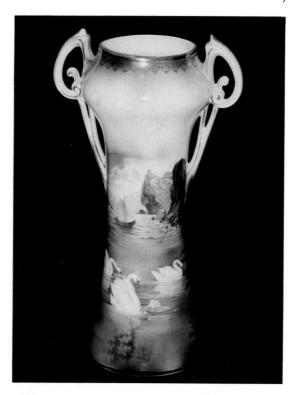

Plate 167. Vase, 11"h, Mold 940, Old Man in the Mountain scene with Swans in the foreground; a single swan is on the reverse side (not shown). $800.00 – 1,000.00.

Plate 168. This and the next three pictures show examples with the Sheepherder 1 transfer. Bowl, 10½"d, Mold 155; shaded green background; gold outlining on mold designs. $1,200.00 – 1,400.00.

Plate 169. *Celery Dish, 12"l, 6"w, Mold 304, a cameo of the Sheepherder 1 scene is combined with the Swallows on an undecorated background. $600.00 – 700.00.*

Plate 170. *Sugar and Creamer Set, Mold 620 with jewels decorated as pearls; the full view of the Sheepherder scene is accompanied by Swallows in gold framed panels on this set. $800.00 – 1,000.00 set.*

Plate 172. *The following six pictures illustrate the Snowbird scene. Oval Bowl, 13½"l, 6¾"w, Mold 7, Icicle Mold. $1,600.00 – 1,800.00.*

Plate 171. *Hatpin Holder, 4½"h, Mold 728; the House view of the Sheepherder 1 scene is visible on this piece. $350.00 – 450.00.*

Plate 173. *Cracker Jar, 7½"h, Mold 641, companion to Icicle Mold; unmarked. $1,200.00 – 1,400.00.*

Plate 174. Tray, 11½"l, Mold 14, Medallion Mold; Snowbird center decor; Sheepherder 1, Man in the Mountain, and Snowbird scenes without Snowbirds decorate the medallions on the border; black finish on the inner border; heavy gold outer border. $2,400.00 – 2,600.00.

Plate 175. Chocolate Pot, 9½"h, Mold 631, companion to the Medallion Mold; black finish at top and base with gold stencilled designs; the reverse of this piece is decorated with Swans. $1,800.00 – 2,000.00.

Plate 176. *Plate 8½"d, Mold 92, Popcorn Mold; the Snowbird scene is framed by the mold design which is decorated with a gold stencilled pattern. $1,200.00 – 1,400.00.*

Plate 177. *Bowl, 10¾"d, Mold 113; white satin finish on Snowbird scene; pearl button finish on sections separating dome shapes of mold; unmarked. $1,800.00 – 2,000.00.*

Bird Decorations
Swans
(Plates 178 – 215)

Swans, Swallows, Pheasants, Peacocks, Ducks, and Turkeys are a unique form of scenic decoration found on R. S. Prussia china. Swans were used as a decoration on the china more than the other birds. The swan, according to legends, is said to have loved music and to have sung a beautiful song when it died. Another legend says that the soul of a poet entered the body of the swan. Swans are graceful and beautiful creatures, qualities which have made them a popular subject for artistic interpretation.

There are several types of Swan decorations unlike most other subjects. Swans on R. S. Prussia china vary in number and in backgrounds. They may appear singly, in pairs, or in groups. The most common background is a blue lake. An Aisle of Swans or Swans and Evergreens show the birds swimming down a narrow aisle formed by evergreen trees. A gazebo and a terrace are two other rather unusual backgrounds for Swan scenes. In the terrace scene, an urn on a column is part of the transfer, but sometimes only part of the transfer was used, or depending on the picture, only part of the view can be seen. A more simple background of evergreen trees than the Aisle of Evergreens is a small stand of pine trees. That particular transfer is found with other farm birds as well.

By looking carefully at the swans' necks, we can see that more than one type of Swan transfer was used by the factory decorators. These variations will be obvious in the pictures as similar ones have been placed together. A transfer of Black Swans is considered rare, and I have placed those examples in the Scarce and Rare section.

Values for china decorated with Swans are somewhat lower than for the Castle, Cottage, and Mill scenes. Prices are higher when the Swans are combined with another subject such as the Old Man in the Mountain or the Snowbird.

In the following photographs, a large variety of pieces with different Swan decorations is shown first. Examples of the other birds follow.

Plate 178. Syrup Pitcher, 6"h, Mold 631, Medallion Mold; a single Swan decorates medallion with Swallows on upper gold tapestry border; FD6, Poppies and Lily of the Valley, decorates the lower half of pitcher. $325.00 – 375.00.

Plate 179. Ewer, 5"h, Mold 640, single Swan. $250.00 – 350.00.

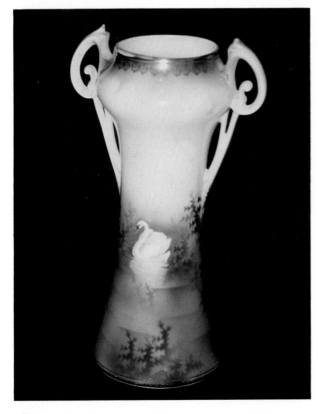

Plate 180. Vase, 11"h, Mold 940; a single Swan is shown on the reverse side of a vase decorated with the Old Man in the Mountain and Swans on the Lake. $800.00 – 1,000.00.

Plate 181. Sugar, 5½"h, Creamer, 4½"h, Mold 540a; a pair of Swans with a Gazebo in the background. $650.00 – 750.00.

Plate 182. Talcum Shaker or Muffineer, Mold 729, companion to Mold 540a; the Gazebo scene is barely visible on the left side of this piece. $275.00 – 325.00.

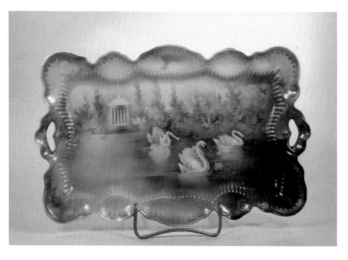

Plate 183. Tray, 12"l, 9"w, Mold 327; three Swans on the lake with the gazebo in the background. $600.00 – 700.00.

Plate 184. Cake Plate, 10"d, Mold 341, companion to Mold 327; Swans with gazebo. $450.00 – 550.00.

Plate 185. Syrup Pitcher, 5½"h, and Underplate, Mold 476; Swans and terrace scene. $400.00 – 500.00.

Plate 186. Bowl, 10½"d, Mold 205; Swans and terrace scene. $450.00 – 550.00.

Plate 187. *Cider Pitcher, 6¼"h, Mold 646; Swans and terrace. $600.00 – 700.00.*

Plate 188. *Ferner, 3½"h, 8½"d, Mold 878, companion to Mold 646; Swans and terrace scene. $500.00 – 600.00.*

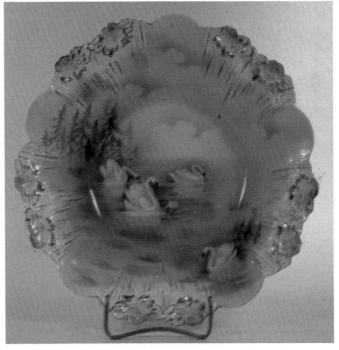

Plate 189. *Bowl, 11"d, Mold 7, Icicle Mold; Swans on lake. $550.00 – 650.00.*

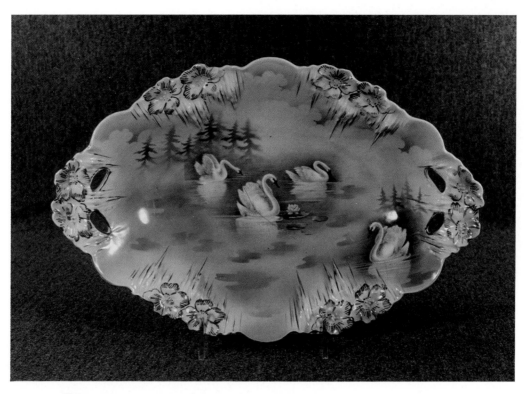

Plate 190. Oval Bowl, 13"l, Mold 7; Swans on lake. $600.00 – 700.00.

Plate 191. Cracker Jar, 5"h, 9"w, Mold 641, companion to the
Icicle Mold; Swans on lake. $600.00 – 700.00.

Plate 192. Bowl, 9¼"d, Mold 155; Swans on lake with one Swallow. $450.00 – 550.00.

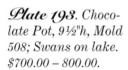

Plate 193. Chocolate Pot, 9½"h, Mold 508; Swans on lake. $700.00 – 800.00.

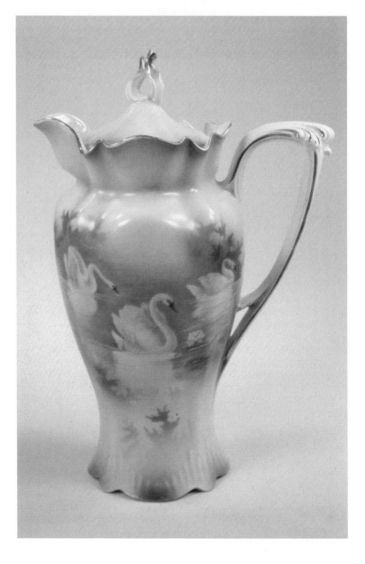

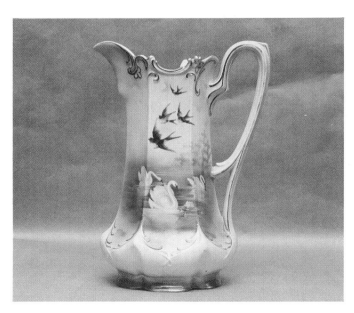

Plate 194. Tankard 11"h, Mold 570; Swans on lake with Swallows. $1,000.00 – 1,200.00.

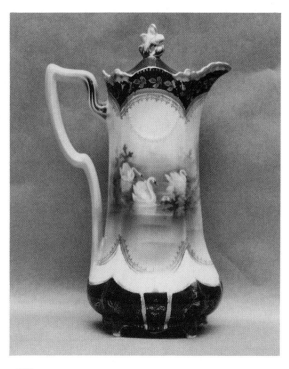

Plate 195. Chocolate Pot, 9½"h, Mold 631, Medallion Mold; Swans on lake; black finish at top and base with gold stencilled floral designs. The reverse side is decorated with the Snowbird scene which accounts for the higher value of this piece. $1,800.00 – 2,000.00.

Plate 196. Hatpin Holder, 4½"h, Mold 728; Swans on lake; unmarked. $400.00 – 500.00.

Plate 197. Ferner, 9"d, 4"h, Mold 882; Swans on lake; gold trim. $550.00 – 650.00.

Plate 198. *Cracker Jar, 5½"h, Mold 633; Swans and pines; pearl luster finish. $550.00 – 650.00.*

Plate 199. *Bowl, 10½"d, Mold 217; Swans through Aisle of Evergreens; luster finish; unmarked. $500.00 – 600.00.*

Plate 200. *Oval Bowl, 13"l, 8½"w, Mold 304; Swans and evergreens; pearlized luster finish. $600.00 – 700.00.*

Plate 201. *Tankard, Mold 584, companion to Mold 304; Swans and evergreens; gold outlining on scroll work and gold trim on handle. $1,300.00 – 1,500.00.*

Plate 202. Mustard Pot, 3½"h, Mold 508; Swans and evergreens. Note that the decoration on this piece was not completed. The transfer does not blend in with any background. $150.00 – 200.00.

Plate 203. Chocolate Pot, 10"h, Mold 641, Icicle Mold; Swans and evergreens decorate the front with evergreens on the back (not shown). $1,200.00 – 1,400.00.

Plate 204. Plate, 8½"d, Mold 92, Popcorn Mold; Swans on lake in foreground with FD36, Reflecting Poppies and Daisies at top of plate; gold stencilled designs and gold trim. $450.00 – 550.00.

Plate 205. Vase, 9½"h, Mold 922; Swans and evergreens; gold trim. $650.00 – 750.00.

Plate 206. Chocolate Set: Pot, 11"h, Cups 3½"h, Mold 510; these Swans are different from the ones in the preceding pictures; light pink background with satin finish; gold trim. Chocolate Pot, $550.00 – 650.00; Cup and Saucer, $150.00 – 175.00 each set.

Plate 207. *Sugar, 5"h, and Creamer, 4"h, Mold 452; satin finish. $300.00 – 400.00 set. In this Swan decoration, there are usually two pairs of Swans. The background of blue water, white shadow flowers, and green shadow trees may have a matte or a satin finish. Sometimes only one pair of Swans or a single Swan is visible. This and the following five pictures show versions of this particular Swan decor.*

Plate 208. *Chocolate Pot, 10"h, Mold 452; two pairs of Swans on lake; satin finish. $700.00 – 900.00.*

Plate 209. Spooner, 3½"h, Mold 521, companion to Mold 452; one pair of Swans on lake; matte finish. $250.00 – 350.00.

Plate 210. Shaving Mug, 3½"h, Mold 577; one pair of Swans on lake. $450.00 – 550.00.

Plate 211. Sugar, 5½"h, Mold 577; one pair of Swans on lake; satin finish. $200.00 – 250.00.

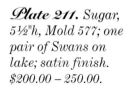

Plate 212. *Sugar, 5½"h, and Creamer, 4½"h, Mold 577; one Swan on lake; light pink tinted shadow flowers; satin finish.*
$400.00 – 500.00.

Plate 213. *Cake Plate, 11½"d, Mold 202. These Swans have feathers accented with a gray-black color; green finish with white shadow flowers on lower half of plate.*
$225.00 – 275.00.

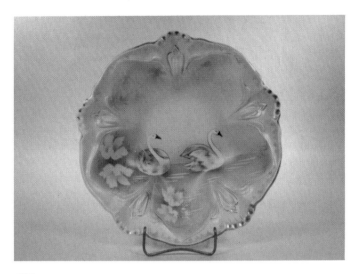

Plate 214. Bowl, 10½"d, Mold 13, Maize Mold. The Swans are the same as the ones in the preceding picture; satin finish and gold trim. $250.00 – 300.00.

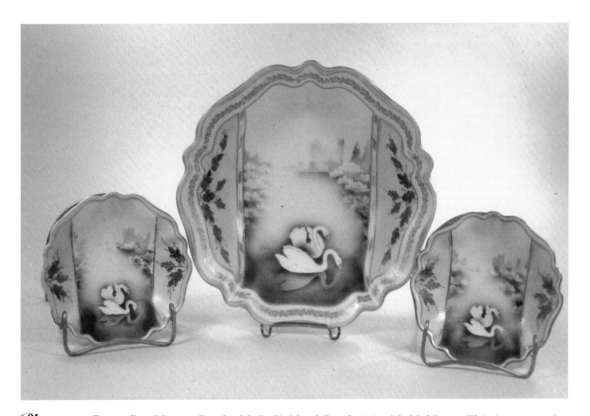

Plate 215. Berry Set: Master Bowl, 9"d; Individual Bowls (6), 5"d, Mold 305. This is yet another Swan scene. Note the reflection in the water of the Swan in the foreground; dark green leaves on each side of the bowls match the color of the water; the scenic panel has a matte finish while there is a satin finish around the design. Master Bowl, $400.00 – 500.00; Individual Bowl, $60.00 – 75.00 each.

Swallows and other Barnyard Birds
(Plates 216 – 243)

Swallows and other birds such as ducks, chickens, peacocks, pheasants, and turkeys are found on numerous molds and pieces of R. S. Prussia. They, like the swans, are usually portrayed in an outdoor or naturalistic setting. These particular birds are also frequently shown together in specific decorations. One popular rendition is called "Barnyard Animals" by collectors. A rooster, chicken, and ducks form a group. Often, a pheasant, sometimes called a Chinese Pheasant, is part of the scene as well. Swallows or bluebirds were also commonly used as a part of other bird decorations.

A rare scene incorporates separate transfers of the Swans, Barnyard Animals, and Swallows. This decoration is referred to as Three Scenes. Some examples are shown in the section on Scarce and Rare Decorations. Note, too that other popular bird decorations on R. S. Prussia such as the Bird of Paradise, Hummingbird, and Parrots are also shown in that section rather than here.

Values for the Peacock, Pheasant, and Turkey scenes are usually more than for the Swans. Lower prices are paid for Swallow-decorated china unless they are combined with some other bird or scene. The Barnyard Animals are usually comparable in value to the Swans, depending on the piece and mold.

Plate 216. Toothpick Holder, 2¼" h, two handles, Mold 631, Medallion Mold; Swallows with white water lilies. $225.00 – 275.00.

Plate 217. Bowl, 11"d, Mold 157; twelve Swallows scattered across surface of bowl; pearl luster finish. $375.00 – 475.00.

Plate 218. Bowl, 7¼"d, one-pieced handle, Mold 181a; Swallows with water lilies; light green background shading to white; gold trim. $375.00 – 425.00.

Plate 219. Sugar and Creamer set, 4"h, Mold 602; Swallows with water lilies; light blue-green finish at base; gold trim. $250.00 – 300.00 set.

Plate 220. Tankard, 13"h, Mold 584; Swallows on yellow to beige background; large white water lilies decorate base; gold trim. $750.00 – 850.00.

Plate 221. *Hatpin Holder, 4½"h, Mold 728; Swallows against a blue sky with white clouds; gold trim. $225.00 – 275.00.*

Plate 222. *Bowl, 6"d, footed, Mold 8, Icicle Mold variation; Pheasant with shadow images of grass and trees. $550.00 – 650.00.*

Plate 223. Oval Bowl, 14"l, 7"w, Mold 14, Medallion Mold; Pheasant with pines; medallions are undecorated; light lavender highlights background. $800.00 – 1,000.00.

Plate 224. Tankard, 12¼"h, Mold 569; Pheasant with pines; gold trim. $800.00 – 1,000.00.

Plate 226. *Vase, 5¼"h, Mold 909; Pheasant on yellow to rust background; unmarked. $500.00 – 600.00.*

Plate 225. *Vase, 12"h, Mold 902; Pheasant with white birch trees in the background; shaded rust-brown background; gold trim. $1,000.00 – 1,200.00.*

Plate 227. *Vase, 4"h, Mold 918; salesman's sample, Pheasant on yellow to rust background. $400.00 – 500.00.*

Plate 228. Toothpick Holder, two handles, Mold 631, Medallion Mold. This Duck is often referred to by collectors as the Indian Runner Duck or Black Duck. Pines are in the background; medallions undecorated. $275.00 – 325.00.

Plate 229. Shaving Mug, Mold 584; Duck with pines; light lavender tinted background; gold trim. $400.00 – 500.00.

Plate 230. Sugar, 4½"h, and Creamer, 3½"h, Mold 702; Black Duck with white birch trees in the background; gold trim. $500.00 – 700.00 set.

Plate 231. Covered Box, 7"d, 3"h, Mold 833; Black Duck with white birch trees and pines; cobalt blue accents the background; gold trim. $300.00 – 400.00.

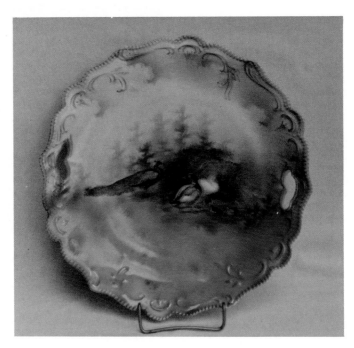

Plate 232. Cake Plate, 9½" d, Mold 304; Ducks with Peacock; rust colored background with shadow trees; gold trim. $700.00 – 900.00.

Plate 233. Bowl, 11"d, Mold 155; Peacock with pines on tinted green background at base with light red finish at top simulating a sunset; high glaze on outer border; gold trim. $1,000.00 – 1,200.00.

Plate 234. Vase, 5"h, Mold 907; the Peacock decorates one side with the Barnyard Animals on the reverse; gold bands form a reserve around middle of vase. $550.00 – 650.00.

Plate 235. Vase, 6"h, Mold 909; Peacock on rust colored background. $650.00 – 750.00.

Plate 236. Bowl, 11"d, Mold 7; Icicle Mold; Barnyard Animals with Pheasant. $800.00 – 1,000.00.

Plate 237. Vase, 5"h, Mold 907; Barnyard Animals with Pheasant decorate center of vase; Peacock (Plate 234) is on the reverse side. $550.00 – 650.00.

Plate 238. *Plate, 8"d, Mold 92, Popcorn Mold; Turkey with pines; gold trim. $450.00 – 550.00.*

Plate 239. *Plate, 7½"d, Mold 304; Turkey with pines; pearlized luster border. $400.00 – 500.00.*

Plate 240. Bowl, 11"d, Mold 334; a white and a black Turkey with pines. $800.00 – 1,000.00.

Plate 241. Chocolate Pot, 11"h, Mold 633; a white and a black Turkey with Swallows; pearlized luster finish. $1,200.00 – 1,400.00.

Plate 242. *Vase, 6"h, Mold 907; two black Turkeys and one white Turkey with green shadow trees in background. $450.00 – 550.00.*

Plate 243. *Vase, 8¼"h, Mold 910; two black Turkeys and one White Turkey; rust background. $600.00 – 700.00.*

Chapter 5

Popular
Floral Decorations

Popular Floral Patterns

Of all decorations found on R. S. Prussia china, floral themes dominate. Floral patterns alone are found on the majority of the production. Floral patterns were also used to embellish other decorations such as portraits, birds, and scenes. More than one floral pattern may be found on pieces as well as partial patterns. Smaller or even miniature versions of some patterns often complement the primary pattern.

Over the years, collectors have coined names for some of the floral transfers. The Hanging Basket, Sitting Basket, Roses and Snowballs, and Reflecting Water Lilies are just a sample. In my Third Series I developed a Floral Identification Chart to point out that other floral designs which might not bring to mind such obvious names as those could also be identified and given a decoration number. The numbers should be helpful for collectors to use to communicate about floral decorated Prussia.

While it may seem at first glance that the number of floral patterns is unending, I found that there is a finite number. I listed 100 patterns and showed examples of each in the Third Series. When I grouped the pictures from all my three books for this edition, there were actually fewer than 50 patterns which are commonly seen. I also studied other references on R. S. Prussia (Schlegelmilch, 1973; Barlock, 1976; Sorenson, 1979; Terrell, 1982; and Capers, 1996). I was able to match my Floral Decoration Numbers to their floral patterns as well as to mine. Moreover many of the same ones were also dominant in those books as those which are shown here.

Depending on the arrangement of the floral trans-fer on a piece of china, the type of background, and any embellishments, the same pattern might look quite different on various pieces. The shape of an object can also influence how a pattern looks. For example, a bowl will usually have the full transfer over the surface, but a tankard might have only part of the pattern, or the pattern might be "wrapped" around the tankard so that only a portion of the full design is seen on the front.

In this section, 40 patterns plus variations for some patterns are shown. They are arranged in order by their Floral Decoration Number (FD#). A description of each design precedes the examples. In most cases, the patterns are on a variety of objects and a number of different molds. You will note that these selected floral patterns are also usually on the most commonly found molds. There will be a skip in numbers in floral patterns shown because the Floral Identification Chart contains 100 patterns and examples are not included for all the 100 patterns. The patterns which were omitted had few examples in my three books. The entire Identification Chart is in the Appendices. Readers are referred to the Third Series for examples of those patterns which are not in this edition.

Values for floral decorated Prussia are generally lower than other types of decoration. That is to be expected because prices are always lower for the more prolific examples of anything. The value of floral patterns is often enhanced when accompanied by cobalt blue backgrounds, satin or Tiffany finishes, or heavy gilding.

Floral Decoration 1 (Plates 244 – 251)

Floral Decoration 1 (FD1) is composed of large full blossom pink roses. Three lighter pink roses and one dark pink rose are the distinguishing features of the transfer. Several buds, a drooping bloom, and a partial blossom are also part of the design.

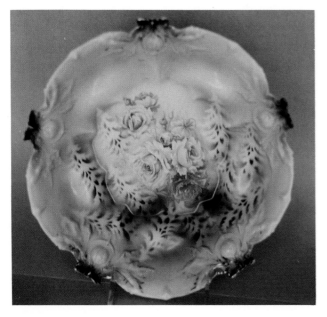

Plate 244. Bowl, 10½"d, Mold 1, Acorn Mold; light blue-green shadow designs form background. $325.00 – 375.00.

Plate 245. *Bowl, 10½"d, Mold 79; FD1 decorates the center with FD7 and FD26 placed in the dome sections around the outer border on a dark to light blue background; gold accents the mold designs and outlines the dome shapes. $300.00 – 350.00.*

Plate 246. *Bowl, 10½"d, Mold 80; light blue-green inner border with shadow flowers; gold trim. $275.00 – 325.00.*

Plate 247. *Tray, 11½"l, 7"w, Mold 23, Stippled Floral Mold; blue-green background with white shadow flowers surrounds floral design; gold stencilled designs around inner border; gold trim. $250.00 – 300.00.*

Plate 248. *Chocolate Pot, 12"h, Mold 526, Carnation Mold; satin finish on body; light lavender tint on molded floral shapes. $900.00 – 1,100.00.*

Plate 249. *Lemonade Pitcher, 9½"h, Mold 526; light green background. $700.00 – 900.00.*

Plate 250. Tankard, 14"h, Sugar and Creamer
Set, 4"h, Mold 526; satin finish. Tankard, $1,000.00 –
1,200.00; Sugar & Creamer, $350.00 – 450.00 set.

Plate 251. Bowl, 10½"d, Mold 211a; a deep rose finish forms
inner border and frames central floral design. $300.00 – 350.00.

Floral Decoration 2
(Plates 252 – 266)

Multi-colored roses, usually pink with one yellow and one white rose, form the pattern. The distinguishing feature of this transfer is the white rose on a hairpin-bent stem. A pink rose above the white one also stands out. Two small daisies can usually be seen at the base of the rose cluster.

Plate 252. Bowl, 10¼"d, Mold 1, Acorn Mold. $325.00 – 375.00.

Plate 253. Cake Plate, 10"d, Mold 25, Iris Mold; a blue background surrounds flowers and decorates the tips of the iris; leaves of iris painted gold; FD7 and FD26 can be seen on the outer border between the iris. $300.00 – 350.00.

Plate 254. Bowl, 10¼"d, Mold 25; green inner border; outer border and leaves of iris painted gold. $375.00 – 475.00.

Plate 255. Cake Plate, 10"d, Mold 32, Berry Mold; a blue-green finish highlights floral design and outer border; gold trim and gold stencilled designs. $225.00 – 275.00.

Plate 256. *Bowl, 10½"d, Mold 55; gold stencilled frame around central floral design; FD26 in reserves around inner border; gold trim. $275.00 – 325.00.*

Plate 257. *Bowl, 10½"d, Mold 94; inner recessed part of bowl frames flowers; dark blue-green finish with white shadow flowers on dome sections around border. $275.00 – 325.00.*

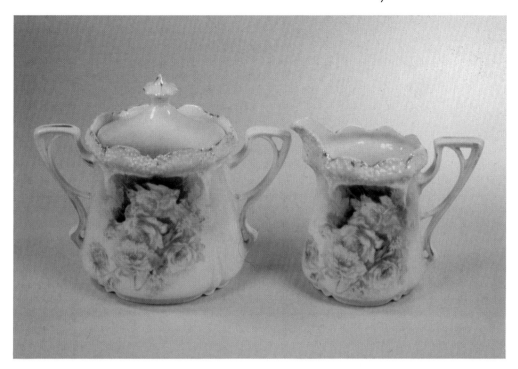

Plate 258. *Sugar, 4½"h, and Creamer, 3"h, Mold 525, Stippled Floral Mold; FD2 highlighted by blue-green background. $300.00 – 350.00 set.*

Plate 259. *Tankard, 14"h, Mold 525; deep rose fading to light rose background at top of tankard. $800.00 – 1,000.00.*

Plate 260. *Tankard, 11½"h, Mold 587; deep rose finish at top and base of piece. $700.00 – 900.00.*

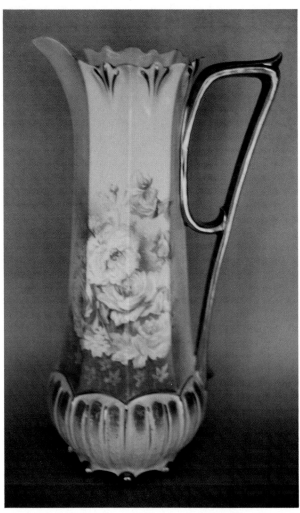

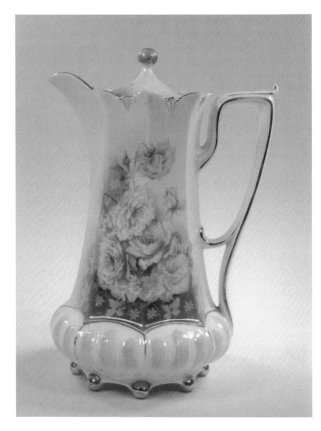

Plate 262. Chocolate Pot, 9½"h, Mold 632 (note handle variation in this piece and the preceding tankard and following Demitasse Pot which are the same Mold); blue-green background around flowers. $375.00 – 475.00.

Plate 261. Tankard, 14½"h, Mold 632, Ball Foot Mold; deep rose finish at base; handle and ball feet painted gold. $750.00 – 950.00.

Plate 263. Demitasse Pot, 9"h, Mold 632; spout and handle are undecorated. $650.00 – 750.00.

Plate 264. Syrup Pitcher, 5"h, and Underplate, Mold 644; deep rose finish at points around border of underplate and lid. $325.00 – 375.00 set.

Plate 265. Shaving Mug, 3¼"h, Mold 644; blue-green background with white shadow flowers. $275.00 – 325.00.

Plate 266. Cracker Jar, 8"h, Mold 644; scroll designs in mold are highlighted with gold. $350.00 – 450.00.

Plate 267. *Bowl, 11"d, Mold 2, Grape Mold; dark green background on lower half of bowl. $350.00 – 400.00.*

Floral Decoration 3
(Plates 267 – 299)

A pair of roses, one red and one white, form FD3. This floral transfer often has another single pink rose as part of the pattern. This particular decoration was used on the floral molds as well as other fancy shapes. It was very popular on Mold 28, the Carnation Mold, as shown in a number of examples.

Plate 268. *Bowl, 10½"d, Mold 18, Ribbon and Jewel Mold; floral garlands decorate FD3 on the inner border; Tiffany finish on the ribbon of the border; opalescent jewels. $300.00 – 350.00.*

Plate 269. *Covered Box, 1¾"h, 1"d, pill or stamp box, Mold 835, companion to Ribbon and Jewel Mold. Iridescent finish on part of lid; opalescent jewels. $120.00 – 140.00.*

Plate 270. Bowl, 10½"d, Mold 28, Carnation Mold; pearlized finish on carnations and border. $300.00 – 350.00.

Plate 271. Bowl, 10½"d, Mold 28; dark green finish on wide border; molded carnations and center of bowl surrounding flowers have a white pearlized finish; gold outlining enhances the center pattern. $375.00 – 425.00.

Plate 272. Plate, 7¾"d, Mold 28; FD3 is scattered across middle of plate with FD27, one large pink rose with one pink bud, on right side of plate; gold scroll work added to the floral decoration; satin finish on carnations. $150.00 – 190.00.

Plate 273. Tray, 11½"d, 7"w, Mold 28; pearlized and satin finish on carnations and border. $350.00 – 400.00.

Plate 274. Shaving Mug, 3½"h, Mold 28; deep rose finish. $275.00 – 325.00.

Plate 275. Syrup Pitcher, 3"h, Mold 28; satin and watered silk rose finish. $275.00 – 325.00.

Plate 276. *Cracker Jar, 5"h, 9"w, Mold 526, companion to Carnation Mold; blue-green background. $350.00 – 400.00.*

Plate 277. *Tankard, 12½"h, Mold 526; blue-green background with white shadow flowers. $750.00 – 850.00.*

Plate 278. *Plate, 7½"h, Mold 78; single pink roses decorate dome shapes around the border; outer border painted gold; "Happ" signature (a factory design painter); R. S. Prussia Mark 6. $250.00 – 300.00.*

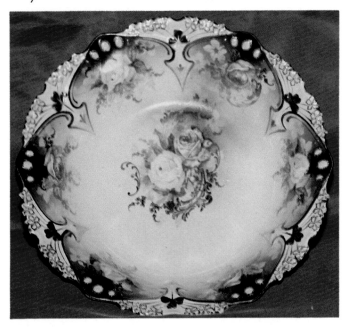

Plate 279. *Bowl, 10½"d, Mold 82; blue-green background with white shadow flowers accents dome shapes around border; opalescent jewels and gold trim. $275.00 – 325.00.*

Plate 280. *Syrup Pitcher, 6"h, Mold 643, companion to Mold 82; gold outlining accentuates design. $275.00 – 325.00.*

Plate 281. *Sugar, 6"h, and Creamer, 4"h, Mold 643; satin finish on body; top and base painted gold with beaded work. $300.00 – 400.00 set.*

Plate 282. Tankard, 15"h,
Mold 643; iridescent Tiffany finish on base. $1,000.00 – 1,200.00.

Plate 283. Vase, 8"h, Mold 939;
iridescent Tiffany finish on base;
gold trim. $500.00 – 600.00.

Plate 284. *Bowl, 11"d, Mold 83; blue-green background around roses and on the border. $225.00 – 275.00.*

Plate 285. *Bowl, 9½"d, Mold 206; iridescent Tiffany finish around outer border; FD3 only on the border with no center decor; gold beaded border. $175.00 – 225.00.*

Plate 286. *Bowl, 10½"d, Mold 201; two sets of FD3 transfers decorate the center; pearlized luster finish on the border. $200.00 – 250.00.*

Plate 287. Ferner, 6½"d, 3½"h, Mold 879, companion to Mold 201. $325.00 – 375.00.

Plate 288. Bowl, 10¼"d, Mold 300, Rope Edge Mold; FD3 combined with a white urn on a pedestal; iridescent Tiffany finish around urn; satin finish above urn. $350.00 – 400.00.

Plate 289. Bowl 11"d, Mold 259, Ripple Mold; FD3 with a separate white rose and a pink rose; pearl button finish. $250.00 – 300.00.

Plate 290. *Bowl, 10"d, Mold 310; FD3 with single pink rose in the center; small transfers of FD3 decorate the wide gold outer border; jewels around border decorated as rubies. This fancy mold also includes large floral designs on border and at base of center pattern. $375.00 – 425.00.*

Plate 291. *Cracker Jar, 6"h, 9"w, Mold 457; dark green background; gold stippled inner border. $350.00 – 400.00.*

Plate 292. *Tankard, 14"h, Mold 537; lavender Tiffany finish on base and around scroll work on top border; gold trim. $900.00 – 1,100.00.*

Plate 293. *Lemonade Pitch-er, 6½"h, Mold 537; gold trim on scroll work and handle. $325.00 – 375.00.*

Plate 294. *Sugar, 3½"h, and Creamer, 3"h, Mold 632, Ball Foot Mold; gold trim and satin finish. $225.00 – 275.00 set.*

Plate 295. *Chocolate Pot, 12"h, Mold 642; opalescent jewel at top; satin finish. $600.00 – 700.00.*

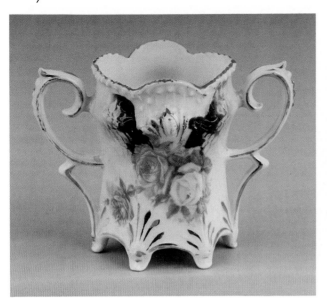

Plate 296. Toothpick Holder, 2½"h, Mold 642; gold trim. $225.00 – 275.00.

Plate 297. Covered Box, 5½" h, 3¾"d, Mold 834; gold trim; RSP Mark 1 with embossed Star Mark. $220.00 – 240.00.

Plate 298. Vase, 7"h, Mold 936; opalescent jewels; lavender iridescent finish at base; gold trim. $400.00 – 500.00.

Plate 299. Vase, 13½"h, Mold 901; opalescent jewels; lavender iridescent finish on base; gold beaded work and gold trim. $700.00 – 800.00.

Floral Decoration 5, 5a
(Plates 300 – 311)

Two large, full blossom pink roses with two similar offshoots make up FD5. This decoration, however, is not as frequently seen as FD5a, which is composed of only the two roses at the base of the pattern. The first three pictures illustrate FD5, and the remainder show examples of FD5a.

Plate 300. Oval Bowl, 12½"l, 8½"w, pierced handles, Mold 23, Stippled Floral Mold; FD5 with a dark green inner border separating the white center and outer border; the signature of "Klett," a factory mold designer, is on this piece; RSP mark 6. $350.00 – 400.00.

Plate 301. Chocolate Pot, 11½"h, Mold 550; FD5 with a dark green finish at top with white shadow flowers; RSP Mark 3. $425.00 – 525.00.

Plate 302. *Tankard, 15¼"h, Mold 517, Lily Mold; FD5 with the dark green finish on upper body; gold trim on handle, neck and base. $700.00 – 800.00.*

Plate 303. *This and the following eight pictures are decorated with FD5a, the base rose design of FD5. Bowl, 10½"d, Mold 29, Lily Mold, companion to preceding Mold 517; the floral pattern is shown in the center of the piece and repeated at points around the inner border; gold stencilled designs beneath a wide gold outer border; Lily shapes tinted light blue; unmarked. $325.00 – 375.00.*

Plate 304. *Celery Dish, 12"l, 6"w, Mold 23, Stippled Floral Mold; watered silk finish around roses with touches of dark green at bottom of pattern and randomly on inner border. $225.00 – 275.00.*

Plate 305. *Berry Set: Master Bowl, 12"d, Individual Bowls (6), 6"d; Mold 28, Carnation Mold; FD5a combined with FD20, a pink and a yellow open bloom rose with one small pink bud; wide blue outer border overlaid with white abstract designs; pearlized and satin finish on carnations around border; gold outer border with inner gold stippled border. Master Bowl, $500.00 – 600.00; Individual Bowls, $50.00 – 75.00 each.*

Plate 306. *Lemonade Pitcher, 9½"h, Mold 526, companion to Carnation Mold; FD5a combined with FD20; deep rose watered silk finish. $700.00 – 900.00.*

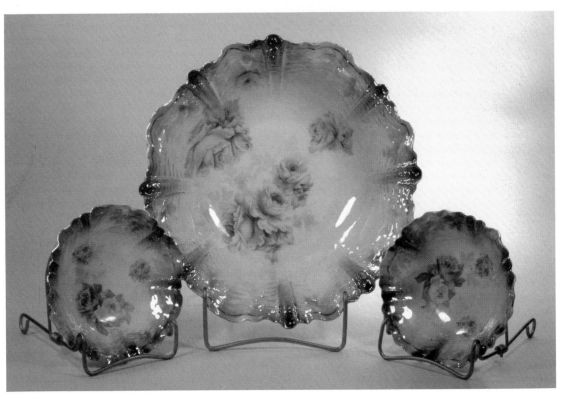

Plate 307. *Berry Set: Master Bowl, 11"d, Individual Bowls (6), 5"d; Mold 259, Ripple Mold; FD5a decorates center of Master Bowl with FD11a, white rose from FD11; FD3, one red rose and one white rose, is the primary pattern on the Individual Bowls; a light lavender accents the pearl button finish on the set. Master Bowl, $350.00 – 450.00; Individual Bowls, $40.00 – 60.00 each.*

Plate 309. *Cake Plate, 10¼"d, Mold 82, Point and Clover Mold; the familiar dark green finish serves as the background for the pattern and decorates the dome shapes on the lower part of the piece. $225.00 – 275.00.*

Plate 308. *Chocolate Pot, 10"h, Mold 536, companion to Ripple Mold; pearl button satin finish. $450.00 – 550.00.*

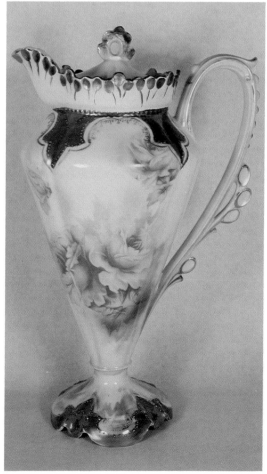

Plate 310. *Dresser Tray, 10"l, Mold 98; a watered silk finish surrounds the pattern and accents points on the border; gold stencilled designs and gold trim. $300.00 – 350.00.*

Plate 311. *Chocolate Pot, 10"h, Mold 608; gold shield designs with red triangular shapes are featured on the top and base of pot; floral designs around top of mold painted gold. $600.00 – 700.00.*

159

Large pink poppies with Lilies of the Valley form FD6. Two pink poppies and one white poppy are the basic pattern. A single pink poppy is usually positioned away from the primary transfer. The small white lilies of the valley are part of each. FD6 is found on some of the most popular molds, such as the Icicle, Medallion, and Plume molds. The background for the pattern is usually white or a light pastel tint.

Plate 312. Oval Bowl, 13½"l, Mold 7, Icicle Mold; small Hanging Baskets, FD44, decorate reserves around border and are connected by a gold chain; wide gold finish over stippled work on border; floral mold designs tinted a light blue. $550.00 – 650.00.

Plate 313. Bowl, 10¾"d, Mold 14, Medallion Mold; single Swans decorate medallions around border; Swallows are also spaced around the wide gold border. $425.00 – 475.00.

Plate 314. Cracker Jar, 6½"h, 8½"w, Mold 631, companion to the Medallion Mold; gold stippled border accented with red triangular shapes; light pink tinted background. $325.00 – 375.00.

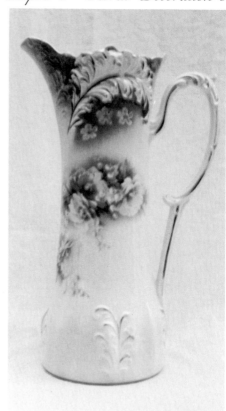

Plate 315. *Tray, 11½"l, 7½"w, Mold 16, Plume Mold; plume shapes outlined with gold; dark blue-green finish around border. $250.00 – 300.00.*

Plate 316. *Pitcher, 8½"h, Mold 465, companion to Plume Mold; deep rose finish at top of pitcher; gold outlining on plumes and handle. $500.00 – 600.00.*

Plate 317. *Demitasse Pot, 9"h, Mold 658, companion to Plume Mold (note base difference between this pot and the preceding piece); rose finish at top and gold outlining. $650.00 – 750.00.*

Plate 318. *Tankard, 11½"h, Mold 526, Carnation Mold; dark blue-green finish at top; gold trim. $750.00 – 850.00.*

Plate 319. *Demitasse Set: Pot, 9¼"h, Cups, 2½"h, Mold 537; FD6 decorates pot; FD81, white poppies with a pink tint, is the floral design on the cups. Demitasse Pot, $500.00 – 600.00; Cup & Saucer, $100.00 – 125.00 each set.*

Plate 320. *Tankard, 11"h, Mold 583, companion to Acorn Mold; rust-brown finish at top; gold trim. $675.00 – 775.00.*

Plate 321. *Coffee Pot, 9½"h, Mold 584; gold trim. $550.00 – 650.00.*

Floral Decoration 7
(Plates 322 – 334)

Two large open bloom pink roses with two smaller blooms compose this pattern, FD7. This transfer also forms the center part of the next floral design, FD8. Single blooms scattered randomly on the surface of pieces often accompany FD7. Floral Decoration 26 is often found as a second pattern with FD7.

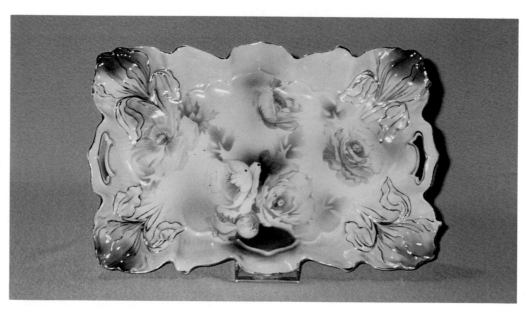

Plate 322. Tray, 11"l, 7"w, Mold 25, Iris Mold; watered silk finish around floral designs; pearl luster finish around border; a blue-green tint and gold outlining enhance iris. $325.00 – 375.00.

Plate 323.
Berry Set: Master Bowl with six Individual Bowls, Mold 28, Carnation Mold. FD7 and FD26, a dark pink and a light pink lily, are combined on this set with a watered silk finish; the carnations and outer border are heavily gilded. Master Bowl, $550.00 – 650.0.0; Individual Bowls, $65.00 – 85.00 each.

Plate 324. *Tankard, 13"h, Mold 526, companion to Carnation Mold; watered silk finish; molded carnations painted gold. $900.00 – 1,100.00.*

Plate 325. *Mustard Pot, Mold 526, FD7 with a watered silk finish; gold carnations and gold trim. $200.00 – 250.00.*

Plate 326. *Bowl, 10½"d, Mold 90; pattern highlighted by a dark blue-green background; RSP Mark 2. $225.00 – 275.00.*

Plate 327. Bowl, 11"d, Mold 100; FD7 and two single blossoms decorate center; light blue finish around border. $325.00 – 375.00.

Plate 328. Sugar and Creamer Set, Mold 583, companion to Acorn Mold; dark blue-green background around center of pieces; gold outlining on molded designs. $325.00 – 375.00 set.

Plate 329. Creamer, 4"h, Mold 605, gold trim. $150.00 – 175.00.

Plate 330. Tea Set; Creamer, Tea Pot, and Sugar Bowl, Mold 607; FD7 on a shaded green background. Tea Pot, $275.00 – 325.00; Sugar & Creamer Set, $250.00 – 300.00.

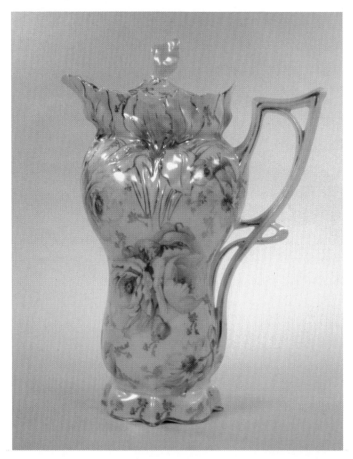

Plate 331. Chocolate Pot, 11"h, Mold 628, Iris Mold;
satin finish with gold outlining. $700.00 – 800.00.

Plate 332. Sugar and Creamer Set, 3"h, Mold 632, Ball Foot Mold; FD7
with single blooms. $225.00 – 275.00 set.

Plate 333. *Creamer and Sugar Set, Mold 707; FD7 on tinted blue background with gold stencilled designs. $225.00 – 275.00 set.*

Plate 334. *Pair of Vases, 5"h, salesman's samples, Mold 910; FD7 and FD26 scattered over surface; gold leaves and floral designs were used to complete the decoration. $550.00 – 650.00 pair.*

Floral Decoration 8
(Plates 335 – 357)

The two open pink blooms from FD7 plus a full, open dark pink rose and a light yellow rose complete the multi-colored rose pattern for FD8. A drooping pink rose is usually an off-shoot from the center cluster. This is a large floral design and thus covers much of the surface of the china. Many of the popular floral molds were decorated with this transfer.

Plate 335. Cake Plate, 10½"d, Mold 9, Fleur-de-lis Mold; a mixed color background of dark green, deep rose, and soft yellow frames the center pattern and the border; gold outlines the mold designs. $225.00 – 275.00.

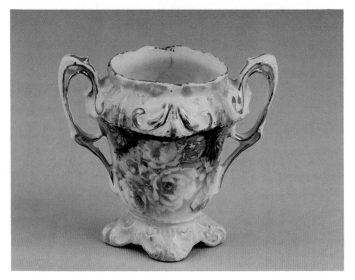

Plate 336. Toothpick Holder, two handles, Mold 609, companion to Fleur-de-lis Mold. $200.00 – 250.00.

Plate 337. Mustard Pot, Mold 609; light blue finish on body with gold trim. $225.00 – 275.00.

Plate 338. Cracker Jar, 5"h, 9"w, Mold 609; tinted lavender background with a satin finish. $350.00 – 400.00.

Plate 339. *Shaving Mug, 3½"h, Mold 609; deep rose background with a pearlized luster finish. $325.00 – 375.00.*

Plate 340. *Cake Plate, 11"d, Mold 25, Iris Mold; background around floral pattern and on irises tinted a deep rose. $375.00 – 425.00.*

Plate 341. *Celery Dish, 12"l, 5¾"w, Mold 25; cobalt blue glaze on wide outer border framing irises; gold trim. $450.00 – 550.00.*

Plate 342. *Cake Plate, 11"d, Mold 25a, Iris Mold variation; irises around border are accented on either side by fan shapes painted gold. $250.00 – 300.00.*

Plate 343. *Chocolate Pot, 10½"h, Mold 628, companion to Iris Mold; dark to light green finish on body of pot. $550.00 – 650.00.*

Plate 344. *Toothpick Holder, two handles, Mold 628. $225.00 – 275.00.*

Plate 345. *Cup, 3½"h, Mold 518, companion to Iris Mold; light blue finish on top of cup. $80.00 – 100.00.*

Plate 346. *Creamer, 4"h, Mold 628. $140.00 – 165.00.*

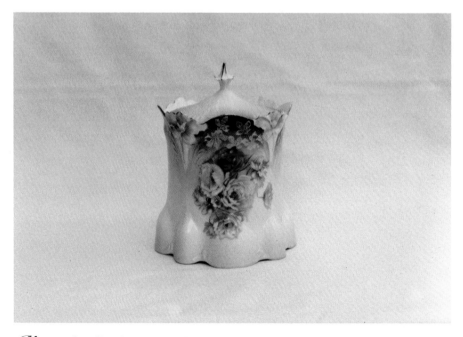

Plate 347. *Cracker Jar, 7½"h, Mold 517, Lily Mold. $325.00 – 375.00.*

Plate 348. Bowl, 10⅜"d, Mold 53a; FD8 is the center pattern with two single roses and one double rose on the inner border; dark to light green finish around inner border. $250.00 – 300.00.

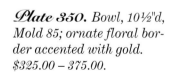

Plate 349. Cake Plate, 11"d, Mold 78; shaded blue finish on dome shapes around floral pattern; sections between domes undecorated except for gold outlining on mold designs. $275.00 – 325.00.

Plate 350. Bowl, 10½"d, Mold 85; ornate floral border accented with gold. $325.00 – 375.00.

Plate 351. Bowl, 10½"d, Mold 211; light blue finish serves as the background for FD8; white and light beige outer border with gold trim. $250.00 – 300.00.

Plate 352. Bowl, 10¾"d, Mold 211a; dark to light green center background. $250.00 – 300.00.

Plate 353. Coffee Pot, 9"h, Mold 525, Stippled Floral Mold; light blue finish above roses and on part of spout and handle; gold trim. $650.00 – 750.00.

Plate 355.
Chocolate Pot, 9¾"h, Mold 644; deep rose finish surrounds molded designs at top of pot which have a light cream colored glaze; aqua tint on feet; gold scroll work and gold trim. $700.00 – 800.00.

Plate 354. *Pitcher, 9½"h, Mold 456; green background colors; gold trim. $500.00 – 600.00.*

Plate 356. *Cup, 2¼"h, and Saucer, Mold 644; the decoration matches the preceding chocolate pot. $100.00 – 125.00.*

Plate 357. *Toothpick Holder, two handles, Mold 644. $225.00 – 275.00.*

Floral Decoration 9
(Plates 358 – 375)

Four large pink poppies compose the pattern of FD9. The distinguishing feature of the transfer is the view of the bent back of one of the flowers which gives it a closed appearance. Sometimes this pattern was thinly outlined with gold as shown in the last picture of this section.

Plate 358. *Bowl, 10¼"d, Mold 2a, Grape Mold variation; four reserves around border are decorated with pastel colored flowers; the alternating reserves are decorated with gold stencilled designs and form a frame for the center pattern. $325.00 – 375.00.*

Plate 359. *Celery Dish, 14"l, Mold 9, Fleur-de-lis Mold; dark green finish around border; gold outlining on mold designs. $250.00 – 300.00.*

Plate 360. *Vase, 9"h, Mold 929, companion to Fleur-de-lis Mold; satin finish; heavy gold trim. $550.00 – 650.00.*

Plate 361. *Cake Plate, 10"d, Mold 10c, Leaf Mold variation; dark green touches around border. $250.00 – 300.00.*

Plate 362. *Oval Bowl, 13"l, 8½"w, pierced handles, Mold 25, Iris Mold; deep rose finish on border; gold stencilled designs form frame for center pattern. $425.00 – 475.00.*

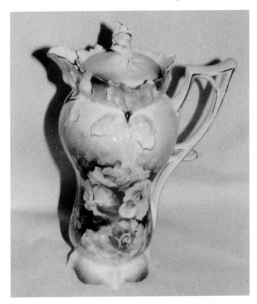

Plate 363. *Chocolate Pot, 10½"h, Mold 628, companion to Iris Mold; dark green background. $600.00 – 700.00.*

Plate 364. *Chocolate Pot, 10"h, Mold 526, Carnation Mold; satin finish. $700.00 – 800.00.*

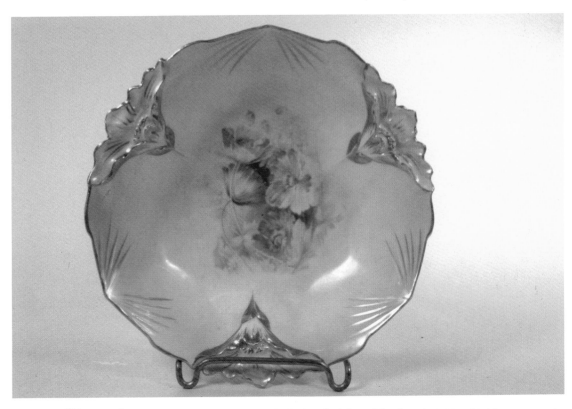

Plate 365. *Bowl, 5½"d, Mold 76; light beige finish; gold trim. $30.00 – 50.00.*

Plate 366. Bowl, 5½"d, Mold 77; light beige finish; gold outlining and gold trim. $30.00 – 50.00.

Plate 367. Bowl, 10½"d, Mold 78; light green finish around center pattern and on dome shapes; gold trim. $250.00 – 300.00.

Plate 368. *Bowl, 11"d, Mold 78; FD9 decorates the dome shapes as well as the center of the bowl; a dark cobalt blue glaze, highlighted with gold, is on the outer border. The rich border color of this piece as compared to the preceding bowl is a good example of how identical molds with the same floral transfer can look so different. $450.00 – 550.00.*

Plate 369. *Bowl, 10"d, Mold 85; light cream colored background around center pattern; light blue finish at points on the outer border and jewels; light pink and green tint on the molded floral outer border. $300.00 – 350.00.*

Plate 370. *Bowl, 10"d Mold 90; shaded blue background; the molded floral shapes of the outer border are tinted a light pink and green with gold beading at their base. $250.00 – 300.00.*

Plate 371. Shaving Mug, 3½"h, Mold 862, companion to Ball Foot Mold. $250.00 – 300.00.

Plate 372. Chocolate Pot, 9½"h, Mold 632, Ball Foot Mold. $375.00 – 475.00.

Plate 373. Ferner, 3½"h, with Liner, Mold 882, companion to Point and Clover Mold. $400.00 – 500.00.

Plate 374. *Vase, 9"h, Mold 944; lavender tinted finish accents cream colored body finish; gold trim. $550.00 – 650.00.*

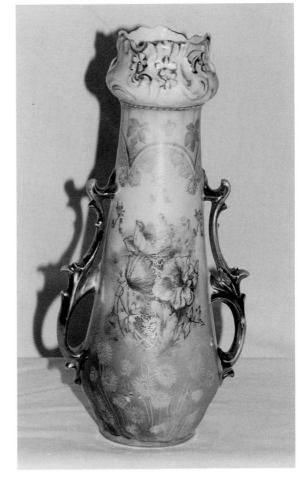

Plate 375. *Vase, 8"h, Mold 955; FD9 is thinly outlined in gold; white shadow flowers on blue to green finish at base; gold trim. $550.00 – 650.00.*

Floral Decoration 14
(Plates 376 – 385)

Two pink roses and one orange rose are the primary flowers in FD14. A pink rosebud to the left of the orange rose and a cluster of white daisies at the base of the roses are also part of the pattern. The stems of the roses are also a distinguishing feature.

Plate 376. Centerpiece Bowl, 15"d, Mold 28, Carnation Mold; FD3 and the dark pink rose from FD3 decorate the inner border of bowl; the white background is relieved with heavy gilding on the molded carnations. $700.00 – 800.00.

Plate 377. Relish Dish. 9½"l, 4½"w, Mold 56; iridescent cobalt blue outer border with opalescent jewels. $250.00 – 300.00.

Plate 378. *Bowl, 10¼"d, Mold 82, Point and Clover Mold; gold finish on border; dark green tint at base of pattern and on dome shapes around border. $275.00 – 325.00.*

Plate 379. *Bowl, 10"d, Mold 91; light blue tint on dome shapes framing center of bowl. $225.00 – 275.00.*

Plate 380. *Bowl, 10½"d, Mold 201; FD14 and FD11a, a single light yellow rose, decorate this piece; deep rose finish around inner border; white outer border with gold outlined designs. $200.00 – 250.00.*

Plate 381. Chocolate Set: Pot, 12"h, Cups, 3"h, Mold 642; FD14 decorates the pot; the cups have the same blue-green background, but they are decorated with FD26, a dark pink and a light pink lily. Chocolate Pot, $550.00 – 650.00; Cup and Saucer, $100.00 – 125.00 each set.

Plate 382. Cake Plate, 10½"d, Mold 300, Rope Edge Mold; dark green glaze on outer border. $225.00 – 275.00.

Plate 383. *Plate, 9"d, Mold 403; dark green background with white shadow flowers; gold trim. $250.00 – 300.00.*

Plate 384. *Basket, 4" x 5½" x 4½", Mold 646; part of the transfer of FD14 is on this piece; gold trim. $300.00 – 350.00.*

Plate 385. *Hatpin Holder, 5"h, three-footed, Mold 726; the floral transfer, FD14, has been placed upside down on this example. $200.00 – 250.00.*

Floral Decoration 15
(Plates 386 – 390)

FD15 is an easily recognizable floral transfer. Its composition is quite complicated, however. The primary pattern of multi-colored roses includes a large light yellow rose and a dark pink rose in the center with two orange roses at the base. Two light pink roses are to the right of the center yellow rose. A white open bloom flower and the underside of a pink poppy are at the top of the pattern. A cluster of three daisies is below the yellow rose. Pieces decorated with this transfer usually have been richly enhanced with vivid borders and heavy gold trim. Jeweled molds appear to have been favored for this floral design.

Plate 386. Bowl, 10½"d, Mold 28b, Carnation Mold variation, touch of blue-green around border with white shadow leaves; gold outlining on molded border designs and gold outer border. $300.00 – 350.00.

Plate 387. Plate, 8¾"d, Mold 82, Point and Clover Mold; iridescent Tiffany finish on dome shapes with opalescent jewels; gold outer border. $250.00 – 300.00.

Plate 389. *Celery Dish, 13½"l, 7"w, Mold 82; red Tiffany finish on domes with opalescent jewels; gold stencilled designs and gold trim. $325.00 – 375.00.*

Plate 388. *Berry Bowl, 5½"d, Mold 82; light to dark pink background around center floral pattern; light green outer border; gold stencilled designs and gold trim. $60.00 – 75.00.*

Plate 390. *Bowl, 11"d, Mold 159; cobalt blue finish around inner border overlaid with gold enameled designs and light pink floral garlands; gold outer border with opalescent jewels. $500.00 – 600.00.*

Floral Decoration 16 (Plates 391 – 397)

Multi-colored poppies in light pink, dark pink, lavender, and orange are found in FD16. The underside of the orange poppy to the lower left of the bouquet is an identifying feature. This transfer can be found with both elaborate and simple embellishments.

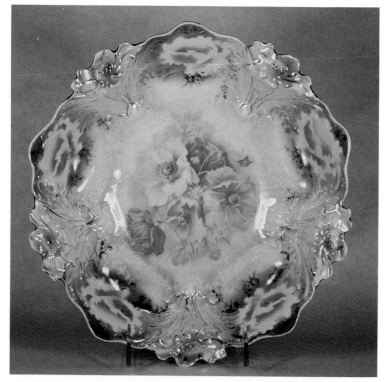

Plate 391. *Bowl, 10½"d, Mold 29, Lily Mold; the highly decorated outer border with lavender or mauve accents enhances the pattern; pearlized luster finish. $350.00 – 400.00.*

Plate 392. *Bowl, 10½"d, Mold 59; an unusual red inner border overlaid with a chain design and gold stencilled designs frames center pattern; floral cameos are spaced around the outer border on a deep turquoise background. $400.00 – 500.00.*

Plate 393. Bowl, 10½"d, Mold 79; blue-green finish and white shadow flowers decorate dome shapes of mold; light beige finish around F16 extending to points separating blown-out shapes; gold trim. $300.00 – 350.00.

Plate 394. Bowl, 10½"d, Mold 94; gold beaded work in center of bowl frames FD16; watered silk finish around pattern; red finish separates gold beaded work on outer border. $350.00 – 400.00.

Plate 395. *Plate, 9"d, Mold 302; shaded green finish on outer border; gold stencilled designs and gold trim. $250.00 – 300.00.*

Plate 396. *Sugar, 4½"h, and Creamer, 3½"h, Mold 632a; blue-green background and gold trim. $225.00 – 275.00 set.*

Plate 397. *Shaving Mug, 3½"h, Mold 644; blue-green background around pattern; gold trim. $275.00 – 325.00.*

Floral Decoration 17
(Plates 398 – 403)

Poppies in pastel colors compose this pattern. The arrangement shows two white flowers in the center; a white and yellow bloom at the top; a drooping orange poppy on a bent stem to the right of the top yellow flower; and an orange poppy at the bottom of the design. The backgrounds for FD17 are also usually pastel.

Plate 398. *Cake Plate, 9½"d, Mold 31, Sunflower Mold; watered silk finish; gold trim. $300.00 – 350.00.*

Plate 399. *Bowl, 10½"d, Mold 202; deep rose touches on border accent light cream background. $250.00 – 300.00.*

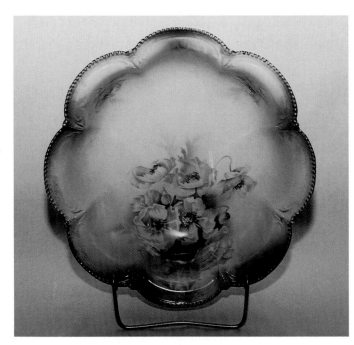

Plate 400. *Bowl 9½"d, Mold 347; light green background; gold outlining around inner border; leaves and burrs painted gold. $350.00 – 400.00.*

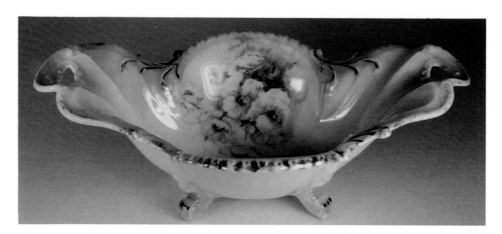

Plate 401. *Footed Bowl, 7½"l, pierced handles, Mold 356; FD17 decorates inner side of dish. $175.00 – 225.00.*

Plate 402. *Cracker Jar, 7½"h, Mold 502; lavender tint-ed background; gold trim. $300.00 – 350.00.*

Plate 403. *Cup, 2¾"h, Mold 627a; pale green, lavender, and blue shaded background; handle paint-ed gold. $70.00 – 85.00.*

Floral Decoration 18
(Plates 404 – 422)

One white open poppy and one orange poppy on a bent stem form a simple transfer pattern found on a number of pieces usually made in the more simple or plain molds. This particular design can be confusing, however. It is often accompanied by flowers which have a similar appearance and color. If the white flowers are viewed very closely, the differences can be seen. I identified one other white flower as FD18a in the Third Series. Here I have added FD18b to identify two other flowers which were used with FD18 as well. Two orange poppies, one on either side of the white one in FD18, are sometimes part of the pattern. Another rounded white petal flower is different as well, and it is identified as FD18c. The various differences are pointed out in the captions.

Plate 404. Leaf Dish, 9"d, Mold 10b, Leaf Mold variation; FD18 on the top border; iridescent and satin finish. $225.00 – 325.00.

Plate 405. Bowl, 11"d, Mold 19, Sea Creature Mold; three transfers of FD18 are at the base of the bowl with one extra bloom; one transfer of the pattern is at the top of the bowl; light green background. $250.00 – 300.00.

Plate 406. *Berry Set: Master Bowl, 11"d, Individual Bowls, 5"d, Mold 151; FD18 combined with FD18b decorates inner border of serving bowl. The difference in FD18 and FD18b is easy to see here; FD18 alone decorates the individual bowls; satin finish, gold trim. Master Bowl, $325.00 – 375.00; Individual Bowls, $40.00 – 50.00 each.*

Plate 407. *Cake Plate, 12"d, Mold 151; FD18 with two orange poppies at base and FD18b in center of plate. $200.00 – 250.00.*

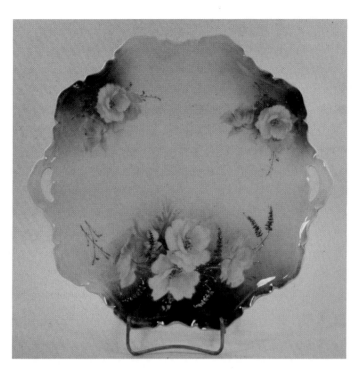

Plate 408. Cake Plate, 12"d, Mold 251; FD18 is located at three places around inner border; on the lower part of plate, there is an extra orange poppy as well as FD18a, a large white flower whose configuration is different from that in FD18; pearl luster finish with Tiffany highlights; gold enameled leaves. $225.00 – 275.00.

Plate 409. Cake Plate, 11¾"d, Mold 301, companion to Mold 507; FD18 positioned in three places around center of plate; gold stencilled inner border; surreal dogwood blossoms on outer border; satin finish. $225.00 – 275.00.

Plate 410. *Centerpiece Bowl, 11"d, Mold 507.*
Note that this pattern, FD18c, resembles FD18,
but is not the same as FD18, FD18a, or FD18b.
The shape of the white flower is different with very
smoothly rounded petals. The orange flower is
also shaped differently. This is an unmarked
piece. $350.00 – 400.00.

Plate 411. *Tea Pot, 6½"h, Mold 507;*
FD18 scattered across body; satin finish.
$300.00 – 350.00.

Plate 412. *Cup, 2½"h,*
and Saucer, Mold 507,
FD18. $75.00 – 100.00.

Plate 413. *Chocolate Pot, 10½"h, Mold 507; FD18 with FD18a. $400.00 – 500.00.*

Plate 414. *Hair Receiver, 4½"d, Mold 805, companion to Mold 507; FD18. $150.00 – 200.00.*

Plate 415. Syrup Pitcher, 5"h, and Underplate, Mold 509a; FD18 with gold enamel work; iridescent Tiffany highlights; gold trim. $325.00 – 375.00.

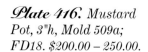

Plate 416. Mustard Pot, 3"h, Mold 509a; FD18. $200.00 – 250.00.

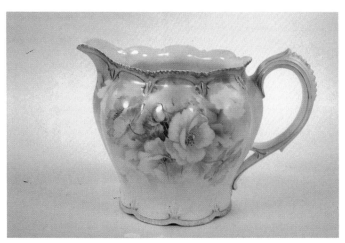

Plate 417. Cider Pitcher, 6½"h, Mold 510; FD18 with one extra white flower and one extra orange flower; satin finish and gold trim. $325.00 – 375.00.

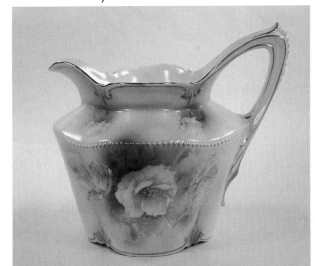

Plate 418. *Pitcher,*
6½"h, Mold 521; FD18.
$275.00 – 325.00.

Plate 419. *Creamer, 3½"h,*
Sugar, 5"h, and Cup and Saucer,
Mold 637; FD18 on Creamer and
Cup with FD18a on Sugar.
Creamer and Sugar, $250.00 –
300.00 set; Cup and Saucer,
$100.00 – 125.00 each set.

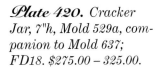

Plate 420. *Cracker*
Jar, 7"h, Mold 529a, com-
panion to Mold 637;
FD18. $275.00 – 325.00.

Plate 421. *Mustache Tea Cup, 2½"h,
Mold 704; FD18. $275.00 – 325.00.*

Plate 422. *Muffineer or Talcum Shaker, 4½"h, Mold
778; FD18 on light cream to amber background; gold trim.
$225.00 – 275.00.*

Floral Decoration 20
(Plates 423 – 430)

One yellow rose and one pink rose separated by a pink rosebud form FD20. Single yellow or pink roses may also be part of the decoration with this transfer because the pattern is relatively small and does not cover too much of the surface of a piece.

Plate 423. Footed Bowl, 7¼"d, 2½"h, Mold 30, Lily Mold variation; single small pink roses around inner border complement the center pattern; gold finish on outer border; lily shapes tinted blue; gold stencilled designs in middle of piece; unmarked. $275.00 – 325.00.

Plate 424. Cracker Jar, 5"h, 9"w; Mold 526, Carnation Mold; FD20 highlighted with a deep rose background. $350.00 – 400.00.

Plate 425. *Tankard, 11½"h, Mold 526; FD20 and FD5a, two large pink roses, decorate piece; blue-green background. $750.00 – 850.00.*

Plate 426. *Cracker Jar, 5"h, 9"w, Mold 664, companion to Mold 98; FD20 alternates with single roses on the dome shapes around the middle of the piece; watered silk rose finish; gold trim. $375.00 – 425.00.*

Plate 427. *Footed Bowl, 7½"d, Mold 98; watered silk rose finish accents floral design in center and single yellow roses on dome shapes on border; molded floral designs on outer border painted gold; unmarked. $300.00 – 350.00.*

Plate 428. *Creamer, 3½"h, Mold 525, Stippled Floral Mold; watered silk finish. $140.00 – 160.00.*

Plate 429. *Cracker Jar, 5½"h, 9½"w, Mold 525; FD20 with FD20a, single yellow roses; blue-green background; unmarked. $325.00 – 375.00.*

Plate 430. *Coffee Pot, 9½"h, Mold 643; single pink roses at base and two small pink roses at top accompany FD20; satin finish; gold trim; undecorated jewels. $650.00 – 750.00.*

Floral Decoration 23
(Plates 431 – 439)

At first glance, FD23 looks like FD18 because it has similar orange and white flowers. The petals of the white flower in this pattern are flat, however, and a yellow center is quite visible. There are two orange flowers on either side of the white blossom. A light orange offshoot on a bent stem drops from the center group. This transfer is usually found on simply shaped molds with little background color or enhancement of pattern. Examples often have a satin finish.

Plate 431. *Cake Plate, 10"d, Mold 151; the leaves of the pattern have been colored a very dark green.*
$175.00 – 225.00.

Plate 432. *Syrup Pitcher, 4¾"h, and Underplate, Mold 507, companion to Mold 151. $250.00 – 300.00.*

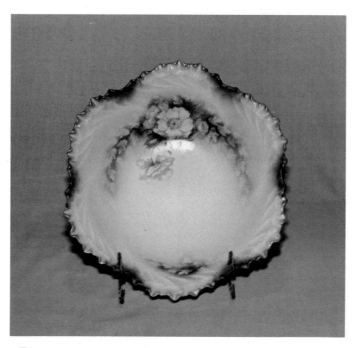

Plate 433. Bowl, 10"d, Mold 212; FD23 decorates top inner border of bowl with small white flowers on either side and at bottom of bowl; satin finish. $150.00 – 200.00.

Plate 434. Leaf Dish, Mold 10g, Leaf Mold variation; light green finish at top fades to white; gold trim; RSP Mark 2. $140.00 – 165.00.

Plate 435. Cracker Jar, 7"h, Mold 503; satin finish. $250.00 – 300.00.

Plate 436. Syrup Pitcher, 5"h, Mold 503; satin finish. $225.00 – 275.00.

Plate 437. Sugar and Creamer Set, 4½"h, Mold 512. $225.00 – 275.00.

Plate 438. Muffineer, 5½"h, Mold 779; satin finish; unmarked. $140.00 – 180.00.

Plate 439. Ferner, 7"h, 6"d, 8-sided, Mold 877; satin finish. $275.00 – 325.00.

Floral Decoration 25
(Plates 440 – 456)

Large white magnolia blossoms are easily identifiable as a popular transfer pattern on R. S. Prussia china. FD25 has two large center flowers. Realistic green leaves surround the flowers. An offshoot, a closed magnolia bloom, may accompany the pattern. Examples with the single offshoot are identified as FD25a. This closed bloom is sometimes found in addition to the full magnolia pattern. The larger open bloom was also used as a single transfer on some pieces.

Plate 440. Cake Plate, 11½"d, Mold 25a, Iris Mold variation; dark green glaze around outer border; gold trim. $275.00 – 325.00.

Plate 441. Centerpiece Bowl, 15"d, Mold 28, Carnation Mold; FD25a, magnolias with offshoot, in center with FD25 around inner border; shaded blue outer border. $650.00 – 750.00.

Plate 442. *Celery Dish, 13"l, 6¼"w, Mold 28; FD25a with a sand-colored glossy finish on molded carnations with gold highlights; dark green outer border with shadow flowers. $250.00 – 300.00.*

Plate 443. *Cake Plate, 11"d, Mold 28; FD25; dark green outer border. $350.00 – 400.00.*

Plate 444. *Bowl, 8½"d, Mold 403; FD25 with closed buds and one open bloom scattered over surface; light rose touches at points on inner border; gold trim. $175.00 – 225.00.*

211

Plate 445. Bowl, 10½"d, Mold 403; FD25; watered silk
rose finish. $250.00 – 300.00.

Plate 446. Relish Dish, 9½"l, 4¾"w, Mold 403; FD25a; gold trim. $150.00 – 175.00.

Plate 447. Berry Set: Master Bowl, 10½"d, Individual Bowls (6), 5½"d, Mold 78; FD25 on dark green background; lighter green finish on dome shapes; gold trim. Master Bowl, $350.00 – 400.00; Individual Bowl, $45.00 – 65.00 each.

Plate 448. Chocolate Pot, 10"h, Mold 452a; one large open flower from FD25 decorates pot. $450.00 – 550.00.

Plate 449. *Cider Pitcher, 6¼"h, Mold 537; FD25 with light rose tint on flowers; deep rose finish at top and base; white handle; gold trim. $375.00 – 425.00.*

Plate 450. *Sugar, 4½"h, and Creamer, 3½"h, Mold 562; FD25 highlighted by a deep lavender background. $250.00 – 300.00 set.*

Plate 452. Cracker Jar, 5"h, Mold 644; FD25; dark green border with white shadow flowers around top middle of jar; light beige finish at top; gold trim. $350.00 – 400.00.

Plate 451. Chocolate Pot, 11"h, Mold 643, Point and Clover Mold; FD25; deep rose finish at top and on feet of pot; white handle; gold trim. $650.00 – 750.00.

Plate 453. Chocolate Pot, 11"h, Mold 644; FD25; touches of blue-green highlight pattern and top of pot. $600.00 – 700.00.

Plate 454. Demitasse Set: Pot 9½"h, Cups, 2"h, Mold 644; FD25; blue-green accent color; gold trim. Demitasse Pot, $650.00 – 750.00; Cup and Saucer, $100.00 – 125.00 each set.

Plate 455. Pair of Vases, 8"h, Mold 949; light beige finish on top part of vases going to a dark green background around FD25; gold trim. $350.00 – 450.00 each.

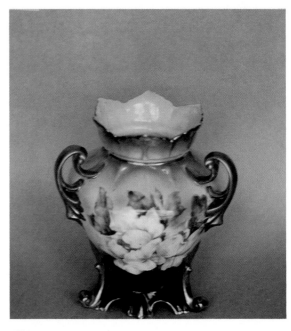

Plate 456. Vase, 7"h, three handles, Mold 950; FD25; light beige background; dark iridescent finish on base; gold trim. $475.00 – 575.00.

Floral Decoration 26
(Plates 457 – 472)

A dark pink and a light pink lily form FD26. This transfer is found on many molds. It may be the only pattern on an object, but usually it is combined with other pink flowers, particularly FD7, pink roses. Smaller versions of the pattern were used as a cameo decoration with some molds. A watered silk finish may highlight the pattern.

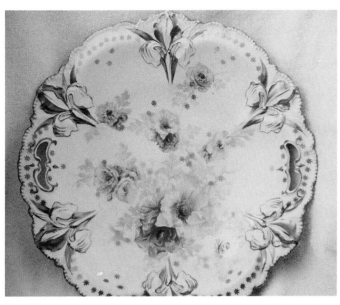

Plate 457. Cake Plate, 11"d, Mold 25a, Iris Mold variation; a large transfer of FD26 is at bottom of plate; a smaller transfer of the pattern is mixed with FD7 and single rose blooms to complete the decoration; iris accented with gold. $225.00 – 275.00.

Plate 458. Bowl, 4"h, 9½"w, Mold 25b, Iris Mold variation; watered silk finish with blue-green color extending to parts of the iris; gold outlining on iris. $375.00 – 425.00.

Plate 459. Cracker Jar, 7"h, Mold 628, companion to Iris Mold; watered silk finish. $350.00 – 400.00.

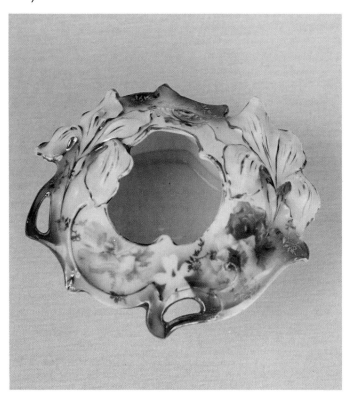

Plate 460. Hair Receiver, 5½" x 4¾", Mold 808, companion to Iris Mold; FD26 decorates left side of piece; deep rose finish; gold trim. $275.00 – 325.00.

Plate 461. Pair of Plates, 7½"d, Mold 28, Carnation Mold; FD26 with single pink roses; watered silk background; molded carnations painted gold on left plate, but only gold outlining on designs on right. $120.00 – 140.00 each.

Plate 462. Centerpiece Bowl, 15"d, Mold 28; FD26 in center and on top part of border; other pink flowers scattered randomly around bowl; satin and pearlized finish. $700.00 – 800.00.

Plate 463. *Tankard, 13"h, Mold 526, companion to Carnation Mold; FD26 combined with FD7 and other pink flowers in an over-all decoration like preceding Centerpiece Bowl. $900.00 – 1,100.00.*

Plate 464. *Cracker Jar, 5"h, 9"w, Mold 526, companion to Carnation Mold; border, handles, and carnations heavily gilded; large and small transfers of FD26 on piece as well as other pink flowers. $375.00 – 425.00.*

Plate 465. Berry Set: Master Bowl, 8½"d, Individual Bowls (6), 6"d, Mold 90; FD26 highlighted by dark blue-green background. Master Bowl, $225.00 – 250.00; Individual Bowls, $30.00 – 40.00 each.

Plate 466. Bowl, 10½"d, Mold 109; FD26 on inner part of bowl near top; green tinted background. $300.00 – 350.00.

Plate 467. Sugar, 5"h, and Creamer, 3½"h, Mold 607; FD26 decorates creamer, and FD7 decorates Sugar. $250.00 – 300.00 set.

Plate 468. Cracker Jar, 5½"h, 9"w, Mold 632, Ball Foot Mold; FD26 on alternate panels of jar; gold stencilled leaves; dark green color accents flowers and round recesses of base. $300.00 – 350.00.

Plate 469. Chocolate Pot, 9"h, Mold 632; pot is decorated similarly to preceding cracker jar except other pink flowers were also used. $550.00 – 650.00.

Plate 470. Shaving Mug, 3½"h, Mold 862, companion to Ball Foot Mold; decoration matches cracker jar in Plate 468. $225.00 – 275.00.

Plate 471. Mustard Pot, 3¾"h, Mold
644; FD26. $200.00 – 250.00.

Plate 472. Chocolate Pot, 9½"h, Mold 645; FD26 combined with one large pink rose; dark green shading to light
green background; jewels painted gold; white handle and
finial of lid outlined in gold. $650.00 – 750.00.

Floral Decoration 28
(Plates 473 – 478)

A dark pink and a light pink rose with green leaves compose FD28. Other single pink rose transfers were used randomly with the pattern.

Plate 473. *Cracker Jar, 5"h, 9½"d, Mold 536, Ripple Mold; FD28 with iridescent Tiffany and pearl luster finishes. $325.00 – 375.00.*

Plate 474. *Berry Bowl, Mold 28, Carnation Mold; dark green finish around border. $50.00 – 60.00.*

Plate 475. *Tankard, 12½"h, Mold 526, companion to Carnation Mold; dark blue-green background accents pattern; unmarked. $750.00 – 850.00.*

Plate 476. *Coffee Pot, 10"h, and Cups (5), 2"h, and Saucers, Mold 526; FD28 decorates pot, but FD3, a white and a red rose, decorates cups; pearlized and satin finishes. Coffee Pot, $700.00 – 800.00; Cup and Saucer, $100.00 – 125.00 each set.*

Plate 477. *Lemonade Pitcher, 5½"h, 8¾"d, Mold 533; dark green shadow leaves form background for FD28; gold trim. $325.00 – 375.00.*

Plate 478. *Vase, 11"h, Mold 930; FD28 near base; iridescent Tiffany finish on base and foot; gold handles and gold trim on neck and base. $450.00 – 550.00.*

Floral Decoration 31
(Plates 479 – 495)

Roses and Snowballs, FD31, were used on many different molds and pieces. The whole pattern consists of two sets of flowers. Two white snowballs and one pink rose with a lighter pink rose offshoot are combined with one white snowball and one pink rose. A blue-green background overlaid with white shadow flowers often accents FD31. Depending on the backgrounds, border colors, and gold work, FD31 can appear either very rich or very subtle.

If you do not look carefully, FD31 may be confused with FD31a. Roses and Snowballs form a similar pattern, but they are in a glass bowl. The bowl is sometimes difficult to see in the pattern. Examples of FD31a follow FD31.

Plate 479. Footed Bowl, 6½"d, Mold 82, Point and Clover Mold; rose garlands decorate inner border of bowl and frame FD31; heavy gold outer border interlaced with a deep blue; opalescent jewels. $325.00 – 375.00.

Plate 480. Cake Plate, 9¾" d, Mold 82; FD31 in center with a white background; cobalt blue outer border outlined with a bright blue color; gold stippled frame work around center and outlining dome shapes. $375.00 – 425.00.

Plate 481. Plate, 9"d, Mold 91; light blue background with shadow snowballs around bottom of pattern and on dome shapes; gold trim around dome shapes. $175.00 – 225.00.

Plate 482. Bowl, 10½"d, Mold 91; cobalt blue finish on dome shapes around border. $375.00 – 475.00.

Plate 483. Bowl, 11"d, Mold 96; light and dark green finish around outer border with dome shapes painted gold. $225.00 – 275.00.

Plate 484. Cake Plate, 10¼"d, Mold 213, gold trim. $175.00 – 225.00.

Plate 485. Berry Set: Master Bowl, 10½"d, Individual Bowls, (5), 5½"d, Mold 329; touches of blue-green around outer border and overlaid with white shadow flowers at base of pattern. Master Bowl, $250.00 – 300.00; Individual Bowls, $30.00 – 40.00 each.

Plate 486. Bowl, 10½"d, Mold 329; light to dark rose background; gold trim. $300.00 – 350.00.

Plate 487. Chocolate Pot, 10"h, and Sugar and Creamer set; Mold 457; FD31 stands out against a dark green background on a mostly white body surface; gold trim. Chocolate Pot, $450.00 – 550.00; Sugar and Creamer, $300.00 – 350.00 set.

Plate 488. Toothpick Holder, two handles, 2½"h; Mold 480, companion to Mold 457. $225.00 – 275.00.

Plate 489. Humidor, hexagon shape, with porcelain lid, Mold 464. $800.00 – 1,000.00.

Plate 490. *Pitcher, 9½"h, Mold 522, Ribbon and Jewel Mold variation; dark green finish at top and base; opalescent jewel framed in gold; gold trim. $475.00 – 575.00.*

Plate 491. *Tankard, 11½"h, Mold 586, Open Base Mold; gold outlining on scroll designs, handle, and base. $650.00 – 750.00.*

Plate 492. Toothpick Holder, two handles, 2½"h, Mold 641, Icicle Mold. $200.00 – 250.00.

Plate 493. Chocolate Pot, 10½"h, Mold 642; yellow-green finish at top with white shadow flowers; gold beaded work around neck; small opalescent jewel. $550.00 – 650.00.

Plate 494. Chocolate Pot, 10½"h, Mold 645, Ribbon and Jewel Mold; light pink border trim with deep rose highlights; opalescent jewels; gold trim. $600.00 – 700.00.

Plate 495. Ferner, 5"h, Mold 881; single floral design from FD31; green pearl luster finish at top. $300.00 – 350.00.

Floral Decoration 31a
(Plates 496 – 507)

The single rose and snowball from FD31 make up the central pattern of FD31a. Small daisies and large white (or pastel tinted) flowers, however, help to distinguish this decoration. A glass bowl holds the arrangement. The bowl has a gold rim which makes it more visible, but it can still be difficult to see on some pieces. The dark blue-green background with white shadow flowers is usually found with this transfer. The examples indicate that this decoration was popular for Molds 82 and 643, the Point and Clover Molds.

Plate 496. *Cake Plate, 11"d, Mold 82; FD31a on a light beige background. $250.00 – 300.00.*

Plate 497. *Bowl, 10½"d, Mold 91; deep rose finish accents dome shapes around outer border which frame center floral pattern. $275.00 – 325.00.*

Plate 498. *Humidor, 5½"h, octagon shape, metal lid, Mold 479; FD31a on shaded green background at base which makes the glass bowl of the pattern difficult to see. $800.00 – 1,000.00.*

Plate 499. *Chocolate Set: Pot, 9½"h, with Cups and Saucers, Mold 608; dark green Tiffany finish on base and top border; gold trim. Chocolate Pot, $600.00 – 700.00; Cup and Saucer, $100.00 – 125.00 each set.*

Plate 500. *Group of pieces in Mold 643, Point and Clover Mold, decorated with FD31a: Chocolate Pot, 10½"h, $650.00 – 750.00; Creamer and Sugar, $325.00 – 375.00 set; Cup and Saucer (10 in set) $100.00 – 125.00 each set; Milk Pitcher, 5¾"h, $450.00 – 550.00.*

Plate 501. Cracker Jar, Mold 643.
$350.00 – 450.00.

Plate 502. Toothpick Holder, 2½"h, two handles, Mold 643. $225.00 – 275.00.

Plate 503. Shaving Mug, 3½"h, Mold 643.
$275.00 – 325.00.

Plate 504. Coffee Pot, 10"h, Mold 643.
$650.00 – 750.00.

Plate 505. Vase, 9"h, Mold 915; dark green finish at top and base; FD31a on light to dark cream backgrounds on middle part of body. $350.00 – 450.00.

Plate 506. Vase, 8½"h, Mold 921; green Tiffany finish at top and base; opalescent jewels; gold trim. $450.00 – 550.00

Plate 507. Covered Urn, 9¾"h, Mold 963, Ribbon and Jewel Mold; watered silk finish around floral pattern; dark green glaze on top and base; opalescent jewels; gold trim. $800.00 – 1,000.00.

Floral Decoration 33
(Plates 508 – 514)

FD33 is actually a group of different floral transfers. The primary one is composed of a white snowball and two pink poppies. Six other flowers usually accompany the snowball and poppies. Sometimes, depending on the shape of the piece, there are fewer than six. The same six additional flowers may not have been used, however. Sometimes the pattern may have more than one transfer of the same flower. This will be apparent from the pictures. The following floral decoration, FD34, was made with some of the same flowers. The snowball and poppies, though, are unique to FD33. Both designs are often referred to as "Scattered Flowers."

Plate 508. Oval Bowl, 13"l, 8½"w, Mold 82, Point and Clover Mold; six other flowers surround the snowball and poppies, but one flower is actually part of another, see at top left and bottom right; a deep red glaze highlights jewels on border. $300.00 – 350.00.

Plate 509. Tray, 12"l, 7"w, Mold 82; again six other flowers frame poppies and snowball, but the flower in the top right corner is different from any in the preceding group. The flowers in the top left corner and the middle section at the base are the same. Satin finish with Tiffany accents around the border; undecorated jewels. $300.00 – 350.00.

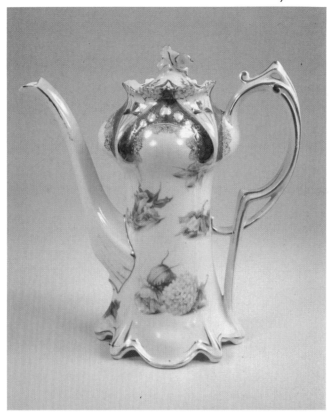

Plate 510. Coffee Pot, 10"h, Mold 643, companion to Mold 82; the pink poppies and white snowball are at the base of the pot with other flowers scattered randomly over the body; opalescent jewels on dark red glaze on border of dome shapes at top of pot; gold trim. $650.00 – 750.00.

Plate 511. Tankard, 14"h, Mold 643; satin finish on body with red highlights; top and handle heavily gilded. $900.00 – 1,100.00.

Plate 512. Cake Plate, 10½"d, Mold 91; only four flowers were used with the poppies and snowball on this piece; olive-green background on sections at base of plate; blue-green finish around outer border. $225.00 – 275.00.

Plate 513. *Cake Plate, 11½"d, Mold 207; opalescent jewels; red accents around inner border; gold trim. $250.00 – 300.00.*

Plate 514. *Celery Dish, 12"l, 6"w, pierced handles, Mold 259, Ripple Mold; high glaze finish; gold trim. $250.00 – 300.00.*

Floral Decoration 34
(Plates 515 – 519)

In this version of "Scattered Flowers," a white water lily is usually part of the pattern. Some of the flowers from FD33 were used with the water lily. The water lily does not appear with FD33, however, and the pink poppies and white snowball from FD33 do not appear with FD34. Two roses, found on both FD33 and FD34, may be the primary transfer or may stand out as the main floral transfer on some pieces decorated with FD34. Both FD33 and FD34 are found on some of the same molds.

Plate 515. Plate, 9"d, Mold 82, Point and Clover Mold; the roses are the focal point on this piece; watered silk background; dark green finish on dome shapes with opalescent jewels. $225.00 – 275.00.

Plate 516. Plate, 9"d, Mold 82; the water lily is the primary flower here; opalescent jewels on deep red border; gold trim. $250.00 – 300.00.

Plate 517. *Sugar Bowl, 6"h, 8"w, Mold 643, companion to Point and Clover Mold 82; roses from FD34 with other flowers scattered across surface; satin finish; red highlights on gold at top and base; undecorated jewels. $225.00 – 275.00.*

Plate 518. *Bowl, 10½"d, Mold 88; water lily with rose in center of bowl on a dark blue-green background. $225.00 – 275.00.*

Plate 519. *Creamer, 3½"h, Mold 525, Stippled Floral Mold; roses from FD34 decorate front of pitcher. $150.00 – 175.00.*

Floral Decoration 35
(Plates 520 – 525)

One light pink rose and two darker pink roses with large green leaves form the primary design of FD35. A second transfer of three somewhat smaller light pink roses completes the pattern. Sometimes pieces are decorated with only the primary flowers.

Plate 520. *Berry Bowl, 10½"d, Mold 2b, Grape Mold variation; FD35 in center; aqua touches accented with gold around outer border. $250.00 – 300.00.*

Plate 521. *Bowl, 10½"d, Mold 88; deep rose finish on dome sections shading to light pink around rose pattern. $250.00 – 300.00.*

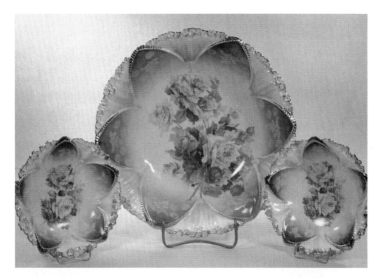

Plate 522. *Berry Set: Master Bowl, 10"d, Individual Bowls (6), 5½"d, Mold 91; the full rose pattern decorates the serving bowl; only two of the primary flowers and one rose from the secondary flowers decorate the individual bowls with the addition of several dark pink rose buds. Master Bowl, $250.00 – 300.00; Individual Bowls, $35.00 – 45.00 each.*

Plate 523. *Plate, 8½"d, Mold 91; FD35 on light cream background framed with gold beaded work; light green finish on dome shapes; dark green Tiffany finish on sections between domes; molded flowers on border painted gold. $275.00 – 325.00.*

Plate 524. Bowl, 10½"d, Mold 201; the primary rose
transfer of FD35 decorates the center on a light lavender
background with a satin finish. $225.00 – 275.00.

Plate 525. Celery Dish, 12"l, 7"w, Mold 207; full pattern of
FD35; blue-green background with white shadow flowers around
inner border; gold trim. $175.00 – 225.00.

Floral Decoration 36
(Plates 526 – 531)

FD36, Reflecting Poppies and Daisies, is a distinctive decoration with need of little elaboration. Pink poppies and white daisies appear to be reflected in blue water.

Plate 526. Bowl, 11"d, Mold 14, Medallion Mold; a wide gold inner border frames FD36; pink and red rose clusters decorate gold stippled border medallions. $375.00 – 425.00.

Plate 527. Coffee Pot, 9"h, Mold 631, companion to Medallion Mold; FD9, another pink poppy transfer, decorates medallion as a second floral decoration with FD36; shaded green finish on base; gold trim on spout and handle. $550.00 – 650.00.

Plate 528. *Bowl, 11"d, Mold 22, Square and Jewel Mold; deep rose accents outer border; jewels painted gold. $300.00 – 350.00.*

Plate 529. *Cake Plate, 10¼"d, Mold 304; deep rose finish with white shadow flowers around inner border complementing colors of FD36; gold trim. $350.00 – 400.00.*

Plate 530. *Bowl, 11"d, Mold 334, recessed center; touches of deep rose around inner border; gold trim. $300.00 – 350.00.*

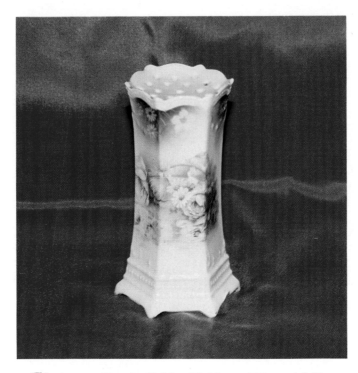

Plate 531. *Hatpin Holder, Mold 728; FD36 with blue-green finish and white shadow flowers around top. $200.00 – 250.00*

Floral Decoration 38
(Plates 532 – 542)

Reflecting Water Lilies, FD38, uses the same technique as FD36 to show the reflection of the flowers. Two large water lilies, with the one on the left usually tinted pink, are surrounded with smaller white water lilies and green lily pads. Usually the surrounding background for this pattern is white, with the exception of the "water." Sometimes, as shown in two examples, the pattern was used with a deep cobalt blue background, making a more elegant decoration.

The first four pictures show FD38 on the Icicle Mold on the same blue-green background with white shadow flowers added to the water.

Plate 532. Cake Plate, 10"d, Mold 7, Icicle Mold. $225.00 – 275.00.

Plate 533. Mustard Pot, 4"h, Mold 641, companion to Icicle Mold; unmarked. $200.00 – 250.00.

Plate 534. *Coffee Pot, 9½"h, Mold 641; gold outlining on neck, spout, and handle. $600.00 – 700.00.*

Plate 535. *Tankard, 11¾"h, Mold 466, companion to Icicle Mold with base variation. $500.00 – 600.00.*

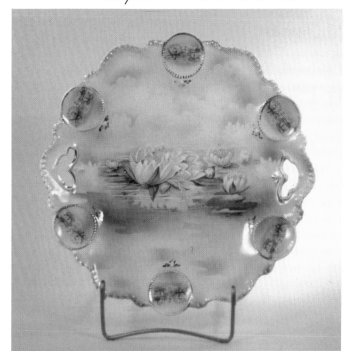

Plate 536. *Cake Plate, 11"d, Mold 14, Medallion Mold; smaller versions of FD38 decorate the border medallions; unmarked. $250.00 – 300.00.*

Plate 537. *Syrup Pitcher, 6"h, Mold 631, companion to Medallion Mold; undecorated medallion. $225.00 – 275.00.*

Plate 538. *Celery Dish, 12½"l, Mold 16, Plume Mold; dark blue "water" surrounds water lilies; scroll work of mold outlined in gold; unmarked. $200.00 – 250.00.*

Plate 539. *Celery Dish, 12½"l, Mold 18, Ribbon and Jewel Mold; FD38 with gold enameling on lily pads; opalescent jewel; light green outer border. $225.00 – 275.00.*

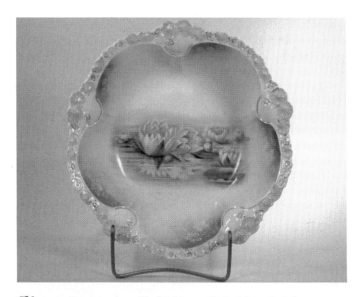

Plate 540. *Bowl, 10"d, Mold 53; light blue finish on outer border; rose tint around inner border. $200.00 – 250.00.*

Plate 541. *Celery Dish, 12"l, 6"w, Mold 304; cobalt blue background highlights pattern; two large white water lilies on left side of dish; gold trim and gold enameling on lily pads. $350.00 – 400.00.*

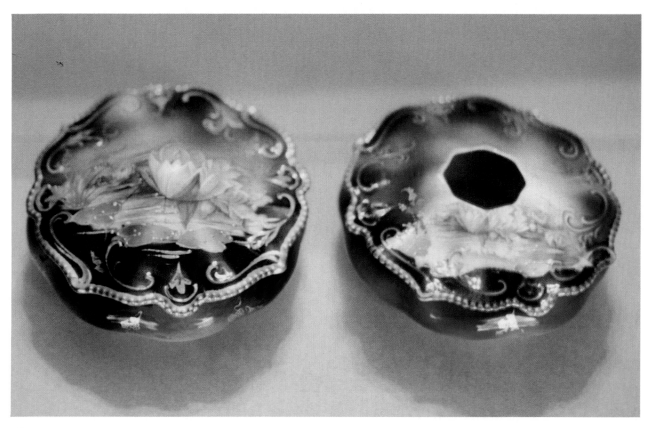

Plate 542. *Powder Box and Hair Receiver, Mold 831, companion to Mold 304; FD38 and cobalt blue background similar to celery dish above. Powder Box, $250.00 – 300.00; Hair Receiver, $225.00 – 275.00.*

Floral Decoration 39
(Plates 543 – 551)

The central pattern of FD39 is made up of lilac or lavender clematis. The number of individual blooms can vary. An offshoot and several buds complete the pattern. A watered silk background may surround the design. Pieces with this pattern may be unmarked.

Plate 543. *Celery Dish, 12"l, 5"w, Mold 29, Lily Mold; light yellow background highlighted with a lavender watered silk finish; unmarked. $250.00 – 300.00.*

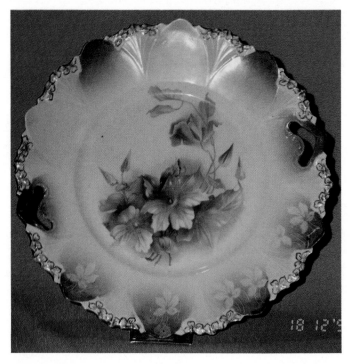

Plate 544. *Cake Plate, 10½"d, Mold 98; FD39 decorates center of plate; light lavender background with shadow flowers around inner border; gold trim; unmarked. $200.00 – 250.00.*

Plate 545. *Plate, 9"d, Mold 205, FD39 decorates the right side of the plate with a single bloom at the lower right; gold trim; satin finish. $150.00 – 200.00.*

Plate 546. *Chocolate Set: Pot, 8"h, Cups (5), 3"h, Mold 459; the full pattern of FD39 decorates set; gold stippled border and gold stencilled designs. Chocolate Pot, $400.00 – 500.00; Cup and Saucer, $60.00 – 75.00 each set.*

Plate 547. *Tea Set: Tea Pot, 7"h, Sugar, 4¾"h, and Creamer, 3¾"h, Mold 525, Stippled Floral Mold; FD39 is the pattern on the lower half of the pieces; a fancy wide gold border separates the top half which is decorated with a green finish surrounding floral reserves of small pink flowers on a white background; unmarked. Tea Pot, $300.00 – 400.00; Sugar and Creamer set, $250.00 – 300.00.*

Plate 548. *Mustard Pot, Mold 525, companion to Stippled Floral Molds; lavender background with shadow flowers decorates top of pot; unmarked. $175.00 – 225.00.*

Plate 549. *Match Box, 2"h, 4"d, Mold 826, companion to Stippled Floral Molds; shaded lavender background; unmarked. $225.00 – 275.00.*

Plate 550. *Cracker Jar, 5½"h, 9"w, Mold 646; FD39 on both base and lid; gold stencilled designs. $350.00 – 400.00.*

Plate 551. *Demitasse Pot, 9"h, Mold 664; FD39 on white to cream background; gold panels around top decorated with gold stencilled flowers; unmarked. $650.00 – 750.00.*

Floral Decoration 40
(Plates 552 – 555)

Light and dark pink carnations form pattern. A small cluster of white daisies is also part of FD40. At the top of the design, an offshoot of a lavender bloom can sometimes be seen, although it may appear to fade into the background.

Plate 552. *Bowl, 10"d, Mold 108; FD40 with a watered silk finish. The offshoot of the pattern is visible here. $275.00 – 325.00.*

Plate 553. *Covered Butter Dish, Mold 108; light yellow background accented with pastel shades of lavender and blue like preceding example; gold trim. $650.00 – 750.00.*

Plate 554. *Candle Stick, 6"h, Mold 853; FD40 on lavender tinted background; a rare marked example of the object. $350.00 – 400.00.*

Plate 555. *Plate, 9"d, Mold 202; FD40 on a white background; gold stencilled designs around the inner border; gold trim. $150.00 – 200.00.*

Floral Decoration 44
(Plates 556 – 570)

Hanging Basket is the name collectors have given to FD44. The pattern shows a basket with a large light pink and large dark pink rose suspended from a blue ribbon anchored by a light yellow rose. Small white flowers with green leaves spill over the left side of the basket. This decoration is frequently found on a large variety of molds and different types of pieces.

Plate 556. Bowl, Mold 7a, Icicle Mold Variation; light blue touches with white shadow flowers around outer border. $250.00 – 300.00.

Plate 557. Coffee Pot, 8½"h, Mold 641, Icicle Mold; a deep rose finish highlights FD44; gold trim. $700.00 – 800.00.

Plate 558. Bowl, 11"d, Mold 14a, Medallion Mold Variation; light blue finish around outer border; touches of olive green on dome shapes; FD44 in center. $300.00 – 350.00.

Plate 559. Cake Plate, 10½"d, Mold 34, Honeycomb Mold; single pink roses decorate dome shapes; light blue finish on molded flowers around border. $325.00 – 375.00.

Plate 560. Cake Plate, 10¼"d, Mold 115; pink roses are on the inner border framing FD44; beige background accented with light blue around outer part of plate. $300.00 – 350.00.

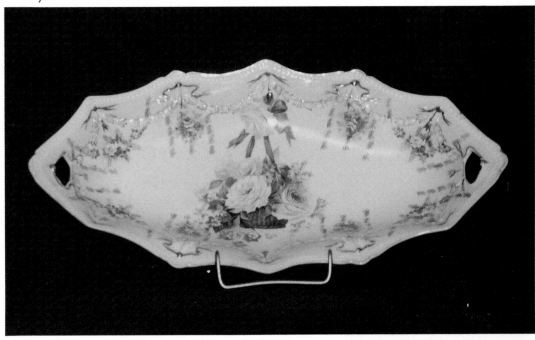

Plate 561. Relish Dish, 12"l, 6"w, Mold 155; FD44 in center on a white background; pink rose clusters alternate with miniature Hanging Baskets around inner border. $175.00 – 225.00.

Plate 562. Berry Set: Master Bowl, 11"d, Individual Bowls (6), 5½"d, Mold 155; high glaze on outer border. Master Bowl, $325.00 – 375.00; Individual Bowls, $45.00 – 55.00 each.

Plate 563. Mustard Pot, 2½"h, and Ladle, Mold 525, Stippled Floral Mold; light blue background at top of FD44. $200.00 – 250.00.

Plate 564. *Tankard, 13"h, Mold 582; touches of lavender accent floral decoration; gold trim; unmarked. $700.00 – 800.00.*

Plate 565. *Tankard, 13½"h, Mold 584; FD44 on white background; scroll work of mold outlined in gold. $700.00 – 900.00.*

Plate 566. *Chocolate Set: Pot, 11"h, Cups, (4), 3"h, and Saucers, Mold 633; FD44 on white satin finish; gold trim. Chocolate Pot, $500.00 – 600.00; Cup and Saucer, $100.00 – 125.00 each set.*

Plate 567. *Powder Box, footed, Mold 836, companion to Plume Molds; cream background with lavender tinted edges. $250.00 – 300.00.*

Plate 568. *Hatpin Holder, 4½" h, Mold 728, satin finish. $225.00 – 275.00.*

Plate 569. *Shaving Mug, 3½"h, Mold 864; miniature versions of Hanging Baskets, FD44, around top border complimenting the larger floral basket. $225.00 – 275.00.*

Plate 570. *Vase, 10"h, Mold 938; light blue border around neck; satin finish; gold trim; unmarked. $550.00 – 650.00.*

Floral Decoration 47
(Plates 571 – 579)

Two large white open lilies with sprays of small white flowers compose FD47. The small white flowers are called either dogwood or maidenhair fern by collectors. They are the same flowers described as "Dogwood" in the following floral decoration, FD48; therefore, Dogwood will be used here as well. One bloom of the Lily pattern may form the decoration on a piece. Single blooms may also be found on borders together with the full pattern.

Plate 571. *Bowl, 11"d, Mold 156; the full pattern of FD47 is on the lower part of the bowl with single flowers at two places on the top inner border; pearl luster finish on inner beaded border. $225.00 – 275.00.*

Plate 572. *Oval Bowl, 13"l, 8½"w, pierced handles, Mold 182; FD47 in center highlighted by a dark blue-green background; single flowers with the same background color around inner border. $275.00 – 325.00.*

Plate 573. *Plate, 8¾"d, Mold 341; FD47 decorates the left side toward center of plate; pearl luster finish; gold trim; unmarked. $250.00 – 300.00.*

Plate 574. *Creamer, 3½"h, Mold 534; single Lily from FD47; light to dark brown background. $140.00 – 160.00.*

Plate 575. *Sugar and Creamer Set, Mold 534; full floral pattern on white background with touches of brown. $250.00 – 300.00 set.*

Plate 576. *Cracker Jar, 6¾", Mold 540a; FD47 accented by cobalt blue finish at top of jar and on lid; gold trim. $375.00 – 425.00.*

Plate 577. *Chocolate Set: Chocolate Pot, 11"h, Cups 3½"h, Mold 546. FD47 with blue-green Tiffany finish at top of pieces. Chocolate Pot, $500.00 – 600.00; Cup and Saucer, $100.00 – 125.00 each set.*

Plate 578. *Cider Pitcher, Mold 554, companion to Mold 546; light cream background; gold trim. $325.00 – 375.00.*

Plate 579. *Cracker Jar, 6"h, 8½"w, Mold 636; FD47 on white background; a single lily decorates lid. $250.00 – 300.00.*

Floral Decoration 48
(Plates 580 – 582)

Sprays of small white dogwood blossoms are the flowers in FD48. I have called this pattern "realistic" dogwood to differentiate between these flowers and the ones I termed "Surreal" dogwood in my first book. From all three books, examples of the realistic flowers were shown only in that first edition and on the same mold. I have included the decoration here, however, because it is part of the preceding pattern, FD47, and because FD48 and FD49 show different renditions of dogwood blossoms. Note that FD48 in the Third Series was not this decoration. I have consolidate old FD48 with FD34 because it fits with that pattern and allows the Dogwood patterns to stay together.

Plate 580. Receiving Card
Tray, 6"l, 3"w, Mold 182;
FD48 around outer border.
$140.00 – 165.00.

Plate 581. Relish Dish, 9½"l,
4½"w, Mold 182; satin finish.
$160.00 – 180.00.

Plate 582. Berry Set: Master Bowl, 9½"d,
Individual Bowls, (5), 5"d, Mold 182; FD48 in
center and around inner border of serving
bowl and only around inner border of individual bowls. Master Bowl, $250.00 – 300.00; Individual Bowls, $35.00 – 45.00 each.

Floral Decoration 49 – 49e
(Plates 583 – 603)

FD49 is called "Surreal Dogwood" because the flowers in the pattern are not sharp. They seem to fade into the background. In the Third Series, I differentiate among three versions of Surreal Dogwood. In this edition, I have added three additional variations. The backgrounds for all but one of the Surreal Dogwood patterns are green. Most pieces also have a pearlized luster finish.

The first pattern, FD49, is composed of rather large white blossoms distinguished by five flat petals and dark green leaves. Small gold dots encircle the center.

FD49a is the same as FD49 except the pattern is enhanced by gold enameled stems. The centers usually are yellow; the color shows up better on some examples than others.

FD49b is also the same pattern as FD49, but the petals are tinted a light pink. The leaves are also a light yellow and not green as in FD49.

FD49c may appear at first glance to be the same flower as FD49. Close examination, however, shows that the leaf formation has rounded edges whereas the leaf edges in FD49 are not smooth. Some examples of this pattern have a light mauve pearl luster finish rather than green.

FD49d is made up of a cluster of blossoms with gold enameled stems and centers. The flowers are smaller than those of FD49 and its variations.

FD49e has a different petal design from all of the others. While the others are flat, the flower in this pattern has cupped petals. The green leaves are small and appear in a chain or garland design.

The following pictures illustrate several examples of all six Surreal Dogwood decorations. The decoration number for each is listed in the caption.

Plate 583. *Cake Plate, 9¾"d, Mold 202; FD49 with gold trim around border. $200.00 – 250.00.*

Plate 584. *Demitasse Set: Pot, 9"h, Cups, 2"h, and Saucers, Mold 474; Plate, Mold 301; FD49 with gold trim. Demitasse Pot, $500.00 – 600.00; Cup and Saucer, $100.00 – 125.00; Plate, $250.00 – 300.00.*

Plate 585. *Tea Pot, 7"h, 8"w, Mold 704; FD49 with a satin finish and gold trim. $300.00 – 350.00.*

Plate 586. *Syrup Pitcher, 4½"h, Mold 545; FD49 with a pearl luster finish. $140.00 – 165.00.*

Plate 587. *Cake Plate, 11½"d, Mold 256; FD49a around inner border of plate on light to dark green background. $200.00 – 250.00.*

Plate 588. *Plate, 8½"d, Mold 278; FD49a on light green background. $40.00 – 50.00.*

Plate 589. *Cake Plate, 10"d, Mold 302; FD49a scattered over surface on dark green border fading to white center. $175.00 – 225.00.*

Plate 590. *Hair Receiver, Mold 814; FD49a with a tinted green finish. $150.00 – 200.00.*

Plate 591. *Cup, 2½"h, Mold 501; FD49a with pearl luster finish. $40.00 – 50.00.*

Plate 592. *Toothpick Holder, 2"h, three-handled, Mold 501; FD49a. $175.00 – 200.00.*

Plate 593. *Chocolate Pot, 11"h with two cups, Mold 501; FD49a with tinted green background and pearl luster finish. Chocolate Pot, $300.00 – 350.00; Cups, $60.00 – 75.00 each.*

Plate 594. *Cup, 2¼"h, and Saucer, Mold 501; FD49b with a light blue-green background. $100.00 – 125.00.*

Plate 595. *Lemonade Pitcher, 6"h, Mold 501; FD49b; unmarked. $275.00 – 325.00.*

Plate 596. *Tea Set: Tea Pot, 5½"h, Sugar, 4½"h, and Creamer, 3"h, Mold 501; FD49b. Tea Pot, $250.00 – 300.00; Sugar and Creamer Set, $200.00 – 250.00.*

Plate 597. *Syrup Pitcher, 4"h, Mold 451; FD49c with a light mauve pearl luster finish. $140.00 – 160.00.*

Plate 598. *Covered Butter Dish, 6"h, 8½"w, with liner (not shown), Mold 451, the underplate is a companion to Mold 256; FD49c with a tinted green background and pearl luster finish. $350.00 – 450.00.*

Plate 599. *Plate, 6¼"d, Mold 256; FD49d with light green finish around border and gold trim. $20.00 – 25.00.*

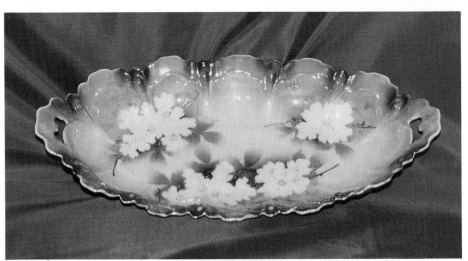

Plate 600. *Relish Dish, Mold 255; FD49d. $80.00 – 100.00.*

Plate 601. *Bowl, 8½"d, 4"h, Mold 335; FD49e on light green background; gold trim. $325.00 – 375.00.*

Plate 602. *Cake Plate, 12"d, Mold 209; FD49e with a satin finish. $200.00 – 250.00.*

Plate 603. *Chocolate Set: Pot, 10"h, and three cups and saucers, Mold 548; FD49e at top and base of pot and top of cups; satin finish. Chocolate Pot, $500.00 – 600.00; Cup and Saucer, $100.00 – 125.00.*

Floral Decoration 52
(Plates 604 – 613)

Three roses in a cluster compose the primary pattern for FD52. Colors may vary from two light pink roses and one white rose to one light pink rose, one red rose, and one white rose. Because the flowers are small, more than one cluster of these roses may be found on pieces. Other single or double roses may be part of the overall decor. The most common double rose with FD52 is a white and light pink rose. Sometimes FD30, a pink rose with another white flower, is part of the design. Satin and iridescent Tiffany finishes were frequently used with this pattern.

Plate 604. *Berry Set: Master Bowl, 10½"d, and five Individual Bowls, Mold 78; FD52 with FD30 and a single pink rose decorate center on blue-green background shading to white toward the center; the double pink and white roses, FD30, and a single pink rose are randomly spaced on the dome sections of the serving bowl; the individual bowls have the same blue-green center, but the center roses vary. Master Bowl, $325.00 – 375.00; Individual Bowls, $45.00 – 55.00 each.*

Plate 605.
Tray, 11½"l, 7½"w, Mold 205; FD52 with a double and a single rose; unmarked. $225.00 – 275.00.

Plate 606. Bowl, 10½"d, Mold 252; FD52 with a satin finish. $225.00 – 275.00.

Plate 607. Plate, 8½"d, Mold 263; FD52; satin finish accented by a blue Tiffany iridescent finish at base of rose cluster. $175.00 – 225.00.

Plate 608. Cake Plate, 11"d, Mold 341; FD52, satin finish. $200.00 – 250.00.

Plate 609. *Tray, Mold 403; FD52 on a light to dark green background; gold trim. $300.00 – 350.00.*

**Plate 610.** *Chocolate Pot, 10"h, Mold 630, FD52; tinted yellow to light rose background on middle of pot with a dark Tiffany finish at top and base; gold trim; RSP Mark 5. $500.00 – 600.00.*

Plate 612. *Vase, 9"h, Mold 944, FD52; lavender to blue Tiffany finish at top and base; RSP Mark 6 (handpainted) indicating the hand-applied gold trim and highlights around flowers. $550.00 – 650.00.*

Plate 611. *Vase, 10½"h, Mold 904; FD52 on a light lavender background with satin finish; iridescent Tiffany finish on base; gold trim. $450.00 – 550.00.*

Plate 613. *Ewer, 5½"h, 7¼"w, Mold 959, FD52; lavender to blue Tiffany finish at top and base; gold trim; RSP Mark 6. $650.00 – 750.00.*

Floral Decoration 55
(Plates 614 – 618)

The floral pattern shown in the Third Series for FD55 is actually the same as FD52, except for the color of the roses. I have placed that variation under FD52 and have identified another floral design as FD55. This particular decoration is quite simple, being composed of large white snowballs. The flowers are usually in clusters of two with some single blooms randomly arranged on the body of the china. The backgrounds are most often in green or brown tones. Thin gold outlining or trim on borders is the basic enhancement for the decoration. The same pattern can be found with the R. S. Germany mark.

Plate 614. Bowl, 11"d, pierced handles, Mold 19, Sea Creature Mold; FD55 with a light to dark green pearlized finish. $200.00 – 250.00.

Plate 615. Plate, 8"d, Mold 301; FD55 at bottom of plate; touches of dark to light brown around edges. $60.00 – 75.00.

Plate 616. *Chocolate Set: Pot, 10"h, Cups, 3½"h, Mold 502; FD55 with enameled work; unmarked. Chocolate Pot, $400.00 – 500.00; Cups and Saucers, $100.00 – 125.00 each set.*

Plate 617. *Cracker Jar, 6"h, Mold 521; FD55. $250.00 – 300.00.*

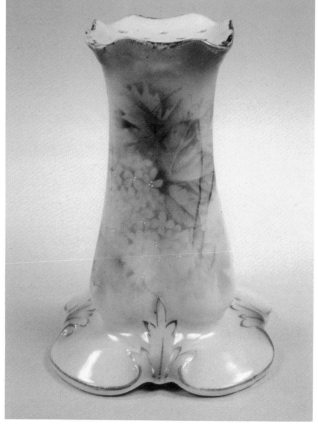

Plate 618. *Talcum Shaker, 4½", Mold 801; FD55. $175.00 – 225.00.*

Floral Decoration 79
(Plates 619 – 624)

The Calla Lily is identified as FD79. Two calla lilies with dark green leaves form the main pattern. Single lilies usually complement the design. Green backgrounds or pearlized white luster finishes are common with this decoration.

Plate 619. Bowl, 10"d, Mold 24, Wheat Fleur-de-lis Mold; FD79 in center with single lilies around inner border; white background with a pearl luster finish. $250.00 – 300.00.

Plate 620. Bowl, 10"d, Mold 277, FD79 around inner border; pearl luster finish. $225.00 – 275.00.

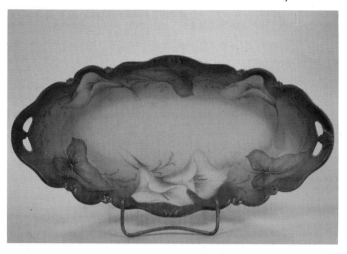

Plate 621. *Celery Dish, 12"l, 6"w, Mold 326; FD79 around inner border on a light to dark green background; matte finish. $200.00 – 250.00.*

Plate 622. *Cup, 2½"h, and Saucer, Mold 509a; FD79 with a green background; gold trim. $100.00 – 125.00.*

Plate 623. *Jam Jar, 4½"h, Mold 475, companion to Mold 509a; FD79 on dark green background around top of jar and on top of lid; gold stencilled designs and gold trim; matte finish. RSP mark with BT Co. Mark (American Importer, Burley-Tyrell). $250.00 – 275.00.*

Plate 624. *Tea Pot, 4½"h, Mold 475; FD55 with same background and marks as jam jar at right. $275.00 – 325.00.*

Floral Decoration 85, 85a
(Plates 625 – 638)

FD85 is the easily recognizable floral decoration, Lily of the Valley. The pattern is composed of a large cluster of flowers backed by large light green leaves. These are usually complemented with smaller versions of the flowers. White satin finishes were popular with this pattern.

FD85 is a floral transfer of Lily of the Valley, but the company also made molds which incorporated the same flower. I have included Lily of the Valley molds with the transfer examples. FD85a has been added to identify that unique mold design. Like the floral transfer pattern, satin finishes seem to have been favored for the Lily of the Valley Mold as well.

Plate 625. *Berry Set: Master Bowl, 9¼"d, and six Individual Bowls; Mold 36, Pie Crust Mold; FD85 with a white satin finish; light gold trim. Master Bowl, $300.00 – 350.00; Individual Bowls, $45.00 – 55.00 each.*

Plate 626. *Cracker Jar, 6½"h, 6½"w, Mold 649, companion to Pie Crust Mold; FD85. $325.00 – 375.00.*

Plate 627. *Chocolate Set: Chocolate Pot, 10½"h, and two Cups and Saucers; Mold 649 with FD85. Chocolate Pot, $500.00 – 600.00; Cup and Saucer, $100.00 – 125.00 each set.*

Plate 628. *Tray, 12½"l, 9"w, Mold 308; FD85 at bottom of tray with smaller patterns at two places around top inner border; touches of brown around the outer edges; pearl luster finish. $200.00 – 250.00.*

Plate 629. *Coffee Cup, 2½"h, Mold 454; FD85 with a white pearl luster finish; gold trim. $100.00 – 125.00.*

Plate 630. *Tea Pot,*
Mold 487; FD85 with a
tinted green back-
ground; gold trim.
$275.00 – 325.00.

Plate 631. *Covered*
Candy Dish, 10"l, 7½"w,
Mold 528; FD85 scattered
across lid and body on a
light to dark green back-
ground; gold trim.
$300.00 – 350.00.

Plate 632. *Demitasse Cup,*
2"h, and Saucer, Mold 660; FD85
on pale blue to white background
on saucer and exterior of cup;
RSP Mark 1 on cup and RSG
blue wreath mark on saucer.
$100.00 – 125.00.

Plate 633. Muffineer, Mold 783; FD85 on brown-tone
background; semi-glossy finish; gold trim; unmarked.
$200.00 – 250.00.

Plate 635. Leaf Bowl, 9"l, 8"w, Mold 10, Leaf Mold;
FD85a, Lily of the Valley molded design, extends from
handle at base into center of bowl; white satin finish with
Tiffany bronze finish at base and gold outlining on mold
designs. $200.00 – 250.00.

Plate 634. Ferner, 6½"h, Mold 879; FD85 with a
white pearl luster finish. $300.00 – 350.00.

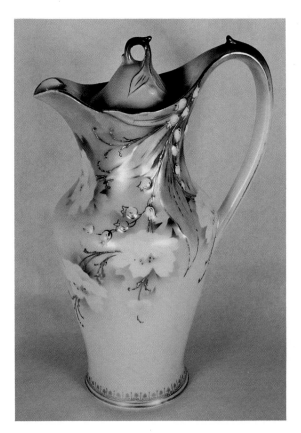

Plate 636. *Chocolate Pot, 10"h, Mold 473; FD85a, Lily of the Valley mold design, extends from top of pot near handle toward middle of piece; FD49e, Surreal Dogwood with gold enameled stems decorates pot as well; light green background fades to light brown to white; satin finish; gold trim. $400.00 – 500.00.*

Plate 637. *Mustard Pot, Mold 703; FD85a, molded Lily of the Valley design, can be seen at base of pot; iridescent Tiffany finish on legs, handle, and finial; gold trim; unmarked. $200.00 – 250.00.*

Plate 638. *Tea Set: Sugar, Tea Pot, and Creamer, Mold 703; FD85a on base of pieces extending toward top; white satin finish on body with iridescent Tiffany finish on bases, handles, finials, and spout of tea pot. Tea Pot, $300.00 – 350.00; Sugar and Creamer Set, $275.00 – 325.00.*

Floral Decoration 86
(Plates 639 – 644)

A spray of four full bloom pink roses makes up the primary design of FD86. An offshoot of two entwined rosebuds at the base of the pattern and another offshoot of one rosebud at the top of the pattern complete FD86. Smaller single roses are usually scattered randomly with FD86. Rich Tiffany finishes embellish the pattern on many examples.

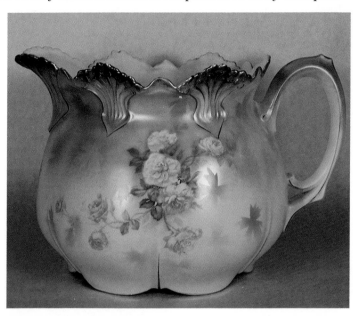

Plate 639. Cider Pitcher, 6"h, Mold 506, FD86; shaded green to cream background with satin finish; gold trim. $325.00 – 425.00.

Plate 640. Chocolate Pot, 9½"h, Mold 552, FD86; brown Tiffany finish on gold outlined leaf designs at top and base of pot. $450.00 – 550.00.

Plate 641. Cracker Jar, 7"h, 6"w, Mold 652, FD86; iridescent Tiffany finish around top border and extending from base in points to frame floral decor. $450.00 – 550.00.

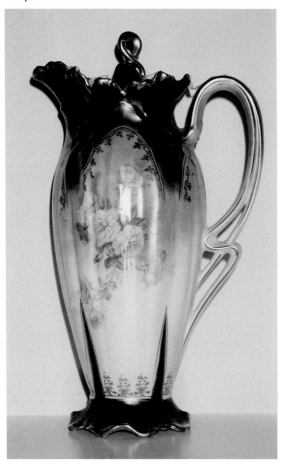

Plate 642. *Chocolate Pot, 10"h, Mold 652, FD86; background matches preceding cracker jar. $600.00 – 700.00.*

Plate 643. *Chocolate Pot, 10½"h, Mold 663, FD86; iridescent finish on top border; molded floral shapes painted gold on top border and light green on base and lid. $550.00 – 650.00.*

Plate 644. *Chocolate Pot, 9"h, Mold 706, FD86; body shades from green to turquoise; gold trim. $550.00 – 650.00.*

Floral Decoration 88
(Plates 645 – 650)

Large white roses are identified as FD88. A group of three roses constitutes the central pattern. Single white roses and more than one central pattern are found on examples. Sometimes only single white roses from FD88 form the decoration on pieces. Other colored flowers do not seem to have been used with this pattern. Brown tones accent the flowers and relieve the mostly white backgrounds which seem to be common with this decoration. Gold trim, used sparingly, accentuates the roses.

Plate 645. Bowl, 10"d, Mold 350; FD88 and white shadow leaves decorate two inner sides of bowl; satin finish with gold touches at points on border. $325.00 – 375.00.

Plate 646. Chocolate Set: Chocolate Pot, 10"h, and two Cups and Saucers, Mold 454; FD88. Chocolate Pot, $400.00 – 500.00; Cup and Saucer, $100.00 – 125.00 each set.

Plate 647. *Cracker Jar, 4½"h, 6"w, Mold 507; FD88 on tinted green background. $275.00 – 325.00.*

Plate 648. *Muffineer, Mold 782, FD88 with white shadow leaves; satin finish. $200.00 – 250.00.*

Plate 649. *Tea Pot, 7"h, Mold 511, FD88; garlands of gold leaves decorate top of pot; satin finish. $300.00 – 350.00.*

Plate 650. *Tankard, 13"h, Mold 525, Stippled Floral Mold, FD88; gold outlining on handle. $900.00 – 1,100.00.*

Floral Decoration 90
(Plates 651 – 654)

FD90, Sitting Basket, is an easily recognizable transfer on R. S. Prussia china. Examples, however, are not numerous. This decoration appears to have been used much less frequently than the Hanging Basket, FD44. A flat based handled basket is filled with light orange and white roses. This is a large pattern and usually is not complemented by any other floral design.

Plate 651. *Cake Plate, 10½"d, Mold 14, Medallion Mold, FD90; gold stars scattered around outer border; pearl luster finish on outer border. $250.00 – 300.00.*

Plate 652. *Tray, 11¾"l, 7"w, Mold 14, FD90; shadow flowers or star shapes around outer border with a pearl luster finish. $250.00 – 300.00.*

Plate 653. *Bowl, 10½"d, Mold 405, FD90; gold stencilled designs with gold enameling frame Hanging Basket in center of bowl; gold garlands of leaves decorate inner border; dark brown finish on outer border; gold trim. $325.00 – 375.00.*

Plate 654. *Demitasse Cup, 2"h, and Saucer, Mold 502; FD90 decorates top interior of cup; light green finish; gold trim; unmarked. $100.00 – 125.00.*

Floral Decoration 91
(Plates 655 – 662)

FD91 is a spray of light to dark pink flowers distinguished by one large white flower. Dark green leaves also dominate the pattern which is usually found on a white background with a satin finish.

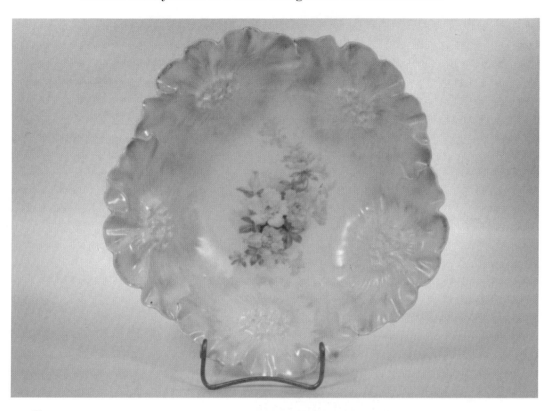

Plate 655. *Bowl, 10½"d, Mold 31, Sunflower Mold; FD91 with a white satin finish. $225.00 – 250.00.*

Plate 656. *Chocolate Pot, 10"h, Mold 553, companion to Sunflower Mold; FD91 with satin finish. $450.00 – 550.00.*

Plate 657. *Bowl, 10"d, Mold 204, FD91; white shadow flowers are around inner border; the outer border has a small checkered pattern overlaid with tiny pink and white flowers. $200.00 – 250.00.*

Plate 658. *Bowl, 11"d, Mold 307; FD91 decorates inner border with part of the pattern in the center of the bowl; satin finish with Tiffany highlights on points around outer border. $275.00 – 325.00.*

Plate 659. *Tea Pot, 7½"h, Mold 473; FD91 against a pale blue background; FD85a, molded Lily of the Valley, extends from top of handle toward center of pot. $300.00 – 350.00.*

Plate 660. *Cracker Jar, 7½"h, 7"w, Mold 505; FD91 scattered around middle of jar; high glaze body finish with a pearl luster border; RSP Mark 2. $225.00 – 275.00.*

Plate 661. *Chocolate Pot, 10"h, Mold 551; FD91 on white satin finish with tinted lavender trim at top; a large cluster of white shadow flowers stands out above FD91; gold trim. $450.00 – 550.00.*

Plate 662. *Ferner, 7¾"d, 4"h (with liner), Mold 879, gold trim. $375.00 – 475.00.*

Floral Decoration 95
(Plates 663 – 667)

The flowers in FD95 are Canterbury bells. The floral sprays have white blooms in the center with others tinted light pink on one side and a dark pink on the opposite side. Small parts of the pattern are usually part of the over-all decoration.

Plate 663. Celery Dish, 12½"l, Mold 205; FD95 extends from base to center of dish; pearl luster finish. $175.00 – 225.00.

Plate 664. Dresser Set: Tray, Mold 205; Hair Receiver, Mold 808; and Covered Box, Mold 832 (Molds 808 and 832 are both companion molds for Mold 205); FD95 with touches of light brown around edges of pieces. Tray, $250.00 – 300.00; Hair Receiver, $150.00 – 200.00; Covered Box, $175.00 – 225.00.

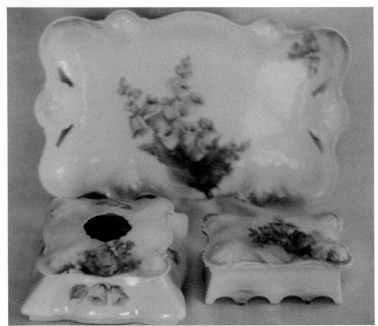

Plate 665. Bowl, 9"d, Mold 254; FD95 around inner border of bowl; touches of green accent pearlized luster on outer border. $200.00 – 250.00.

Plate 666. Lemonade Pitcher, 6½"h, 9"d, Mold 579; FD95 at top of pitcher extending toward base. $350.00 – 400.00.

Plate 667. Cracker Jar, 5½"h, 9"w, Mold 646; FD95 around top of jar and on lid with touches of light pink accenting flowers. $325.00 – 375.00.

Floral Decoration 97
(Plates 668 – 678)

FD97 is called Dogwood and Pine by collectors. Large white flowers with yellow centers and branches of green pine needles form the pattern. The primary pattern consists of three flowers, but some small buds may also be included. One or two of the flowers may sometimes be found as the decoration rather than the main transfer.

Plate 668. *Bowl, 10"d, Mold 203; FD97 on lower part of plate with pine needles at two places on top inner border. $225.00 – 275.00.*

Plate 669. *Cake Plate, 11½"d, Mold 265; one flower and the complete pattern of FD95 decorate plate with a light blue-green background shading to the white center. $300.00 – 350.00.*

Plate 670. *Celery Dish, 12½"l, 6¼"w, Mold 276; two flowers of FD97 are in the center. $300.00 – 350.00.*

Plate 671. Salt Shaker, 2"h, Mold 529, companion to Mold 276; one flower of FD97; unmarked. $175.00 – 225.00.

Plate 672. Mustard Pot, 4"h, Mold 529; two flowers of FD97 decorate piece. $200.00 – 250.00.

Plate 673. Chocolate Set: Pot, 11"h, six Cups, 3½"h, and Saucers; Mold 529; FD97. Chocolate Pot, $550.00 – 650.00; Cup and Saucer, $100.00 – 125.00 each set.

Plate 674. *Demitasse Pot, 9"h, Mold 474; two flowers from FD97 decorate front of pot. $600.00 – 700.00.*

Plate 675*. Cracker Jar, 8½"h, Mold 635; two flowers from FD97 are on the jar and lid. $350.00 – 400.00.*

Plate 676. Hair Receiver, 4"d, Mold 635; one flower from FD97 on jar and lid. $175.00 – 225.00.

Plate 677. Ferner, 4½" h, Mold 880, companion to Mold 635, FD97. $350.00 – 400.00.

Plate 678. Muffineer, 4¾"h, Mold 780; one flower from FD97; unmarked. $200.00 – 250.00.

Chapter 6

Scarce and Rare Decorations

Animal Decorations
(Plates 679 – 685)

The rarest types of decoration on R. S. Prussia china are animal transfers such as tigers, lions, gazelles, and giraffes. Most of these pieces are owned by advanced collectors and are not easily available to purchase. The highest prices are paid for these examples.

Because of the values, copies and reproductions have been made. An authentic R. S. Prussia mark does not guarantee that the animal decoration is one put on by the factory. A skilled artist would be able to add a lion or tiger to the undecorated part of a genuinely marked piece of china. Because factory decorated pieces often employed several transfers or decorative themes, a piece with an animal and some other decoration might not appear out of character at first glance.

If the animal is handpainted, you can be certain that the piece was not decorated at the factory. The factory used transfers of animals. If the animal is a transfer, however, inspect the background coloring and finishes carefully. Are the colors subtle? Do they blend together and fit the theme? Feel of the animal design to be sure it is not a new stick-on type decal.

Other china factories of the era also used the same or similar animal themes. Many of the animal decorated pieces are unmarked. But animals should be on recognizable R. S. Prussia molds and incorporate backgrounds and finishes used by the company. In my Second Series, page 186, I show two unmarked vases. One is decorated with tigers and the other with lions. The mold, however, is one which is identified with the R. S. Suhl or R. S. Poland mark. Thus, the examples were placed under R. S. Suhl rather than with the R. S. Prussia photographs.

From the several examples shown here which are marked, it is easy to see how the molds and backgrounds for the animal decorated china are consistent with other R. S. Prussia marked china. The molds are well known, and the backgrounds reflect natural settings for the animals in the familiar brown or green tones. Little, if any embellishment was added to these decorations. Thin gold trim may have been used on some pieces.

"The Stag" is not quite as rare a decoration as the jungle animals. This transfer is based on a painting by an English artist, Sir Edwin Landseer (1802 – 1873) entitled "Monarch of the Glen." Sir Landseer's animal subjects were quite popular and copied by many print makers. He was a favorite of Queen Victoria and is known to have painted her portrait as well as portraits of her dogs! The Queen knighted Landseer in 1860. Two examples of the Stag are shown here with the jungle animals. The same version of the Stag is found on OS (Oscar Schlegelmilch) china.

Remember all animal decorations should be inspected with the utmost scrutiny. Above all, be wary of the price. If the item is too cheap, you can be sure that it is a copy or a reproduction. Pieces with a genuine RSP mark have the highest value. (For further study of animal themes on R. S. Prussia, see Plate 16 in *The Treasures of R. S. Prussia*, 1976, by George E. and Eileen Barlock.)

Plate 679. *Compote, 7½"d on pedestal base (not visible), Mold 341; Gazelles on brown-tone background. $5,000.00 – 6,000.00.*

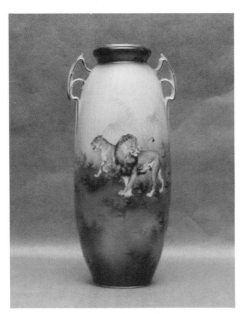

Plate 680 . *Vase, 11"h, Mold 937; Lion and Lioness decor. $12,000.00 – 15,000.00.*

Plate 681. *Vase, 8½"h, Mold 922; Lion and Lioness. $10,00.00 – 12,000.00.*

Plate 682. *Cake Plate, 10½"d, Mold 341; pair of Tigers. $9,000.00 – 11,000.00.*

Plate 683. *Tankard, 11½"h, Mold 537; pair of Tigers; dark brown to cream background; scroll work outlined in gold. $12,00.00 – 15,000.00.*

Plate 684. Bowl, 11"d, Mold 203; Stag scene; satin finish; gold trim. $1,500.00 – 2,500.00.

Plate 685. Berry Bowl, 5½"d, Mold 256; Stag with a dark green finish around part of inner border overlaid with white shadow flowers; gold trim. $200.00 – 300.00.

Plate 686. *Plate, 8½"d, Mold 261; Bird of Paradise.*
$2,500.00 – 3,000.00.

Exotic and Scarce Bird Decorations
(Plates 686 – 702)

The Bird of Paradise, Hummingbird, Ostrich, Parrots, Quail, Sand Snipe, Snow Geese, Water or Marsh Bird, and Black Swans are examples of exotic and scarce bird decorations found on R. S. Prussia china. These subjects, are relatively scarce. Evidently, for whatever reasons, the factory did not use these decorations as much as others. This could have been because they may not have sold well or simply just a company decision to change to some other theme. At any rate, because few pieces are found with these birds, they are prized by collectors. The familiar natural looking brown or green colors furnish the backgrounds for the majority of pieces. Like the animal decorated china, little enhancement was added.

The Bird of Paradise, Hummingbird, Ostrich, and Parrots are found on both marked and unmarked molds. The Bird of Paradise and Parrots sometimes have an R. S. Germany mark. Some examples of the Hummingbird and Ostrich are shown in my Fourth Series under the R. S. Suhl section. These pieces were unmarked, but they were on molds attributed to the R. S. Suhl mark. The pictures shown here either have an R. S. Prussia mark or, if unmarked, are on R. S. Prussia molds.

Plate 687. *Vase, 8½"h, Mold 901; Bird of Paradise. $3,000.00 – 4,000.00.*

Plate 688. *Ewer, 7½"h, Mold 958; Bird of Paradise with a white satin finish. $3,000.00 – 4,000.00.*

Plate 689. *Pin Box, 3"sq., Mold 830; Bird of Paradise. $1,200.00 – 1,500.00.*

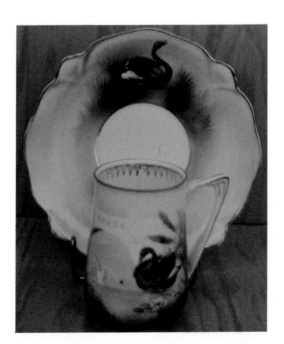

Plate 690. *Demitasse Cup and Saucer, Mold 469; Black Swan on Saucer and Black and White Swans on Cup. $500.00 – 600.00.*

Plate 691. *Vase, 4"h, salesman's sample, Mold 909; Black Swans with cattails, unmarked. $600.00 – 700.00.*

Plate 692. Berry Bowl, 5¼"d, Mold 182; Hummingbirds. $500.00 – 600.00.

Plate 694. Vase, 6"h, Mold 928; Hummingbirds. $3,500.00 – 4,000.00.

Plate 693. Demitasse Pot, 9½"h, Mold 540; Hummingbirds. $3,000.00 – 4,000.00.

Plate 695. Vase, 6"h, Mold 935; Hummingbirds. $3,500.00 – 4,000.00.

Plate 696. Vase, 5"h, Mold 907; Ostriches; unmarked. $1,500.00 – 2,000.00.

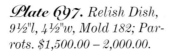

Plate 697. *Relish Dish, 9½"l, 4½"w, Mold 182; Parrots. $1,500.00 – 2,000.00.*

Plate 698. *Tea Set: Sugar, Tea Pot, and Creamer, Mold 576; Parrots. Tea Pot, $3,000.00 – 4,000.00; Sugar and Creamer Set, $1,500.00 – 2,000.00.*

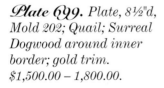

Plate 699. *Plate, 8½"d, Mold 202; Quail; Surreal Dogwood around inner border; gold trim. $1,500.00 – 1,800.00.*

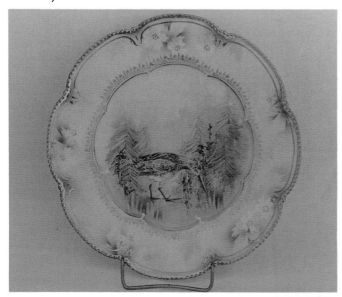

Plate 700. Plate, 8½"d, Mold 202; Sand Snipe with the same background as the Quail. $1,500.00 – 1,800.00.

Plate 701. Cake Plate, 10"d, Mold 202; Snow Geese; background decoration is similar to the preceding Quail and Sand Snipe; unmarked. $1,800.00 – 2,000.00.

Plate 702. Plate 8½"d, Mold 306; Water or Marsh Bird; gold stencilled designs around inner and outer borders; $1,500.00 – 1,800.00.

Fruit Decorations
(Plates 703 – 718)

Fruit patterns on R. S. Prussia are considered scarce decorative themes. It would seem that a lot of china would have been decorated with fruit because so much R. S. Prussia is table china. Of course, examples could be scarce because those pieces were really used and did not survive over time. Several versions of Fruit designs are found; I have divided them into separate categories from I through VI to identify the different ones. The identifying fruits for each are noted in the captions. The patterns are large and cover most of an object. The fruit decor is generally enhanced only by a complementary background color with shadow flowers just around the fruit. Fruit decorated china, though scarce, is usually not higher in value than floral decorated china.

Plate 703. *Oval Bowl, 12½"l, 7½"w, pierced handles, Mold 23, Stippled Floral Mold; Fruit I, peaches with white and purple grapes; single roses around center pattern.* $350.00 – 400.00.

Plate 704. *Bowl, 10"d, Mold 55; Fruit I on a tinted pink background.* $325.00 – 375.00.

Plate 705. *Cake Plate, 10"d, Mold 268; Fruit I with a blue-green background. $325.00 – 375.00.*

Plate 706. *Tankard, 12"h, Mold 586; Fruit I on a dark green and light cream colored background; gold trim. $650.00 – 750.00.*

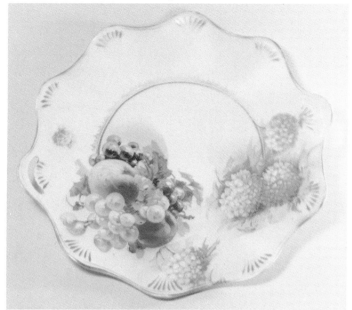

Plate 707. Cake Plate, 12"d, Mold 278; Fruit I combined with FD55, white Snowballs. There is also a faint image of a coffee pot in the center of the plate (not visible in picture). $450.00 – 550.00.

Plate 708. Creamer, 3½"d, Mold 538; Fruit I decor with a variation on the placement of the white grapes. $150.00 – 200.00.

Plate 709. Bowl, 10"d, Mold 9, Fleur-de-lis Mold; Fruit II decoration, apples with red cherries and purple grapes. $325.00 – 375.00.

Plate 710. *Bowl, 10½"d, Mold 116; Fruit II on light blue background; dark blue finish around dome shapes; gold trim. $325.00 – 375.00*

Plate 711. *Cracker Jar, 3½"h, 9"w, Mold 525, Stippled Floral Mold; Fruit II; unmarked. $400.00 – 500.00.*

Plate 712. Chocolate Pot, 11"h, Mold 628, Iris Mold; Fruit II. $550.00 – 650.00.

Plate 713. Bowl, 8½"d, Mold 182; Fruit III, three pears, branches and leaves; light blue-green background with pearl luster finish; unmarked. $250.00 – 300.00.

Plate 714. Cake Plate, 10"d, Mold 182; Fruit IV, a pear, peach, and red and blue berries; light yellow background changing to dark brown; unmarked. $325.00 – 375.00.

Plate 715. Sugar, 4½"h, and Creamer, 3½"h, Mold 565; Fruit V, pears and purple grapes. $275.00 – 325.00 set.

Plate 716. *Bowl, 10¼"d, Mold 257a; Fruit V on lower left of plate; the champagne glass in the center makes this an unusual decoration. $350.00 – 400.00.*

Plate 717. *Cracker Jar, Mold 540a; Fruit VI, a sliced orange with purple grapes; unmarked. $450.00 – 550.00.*

Plate 718. *Lemonade Pitcher, Mold 655; Fruit VI; unmarked. $400.00 – 500.00.*

Figural Decorations

Diana The Huntress and Flora
(Plates 719 – 729)

Diana the Huntress and Flora are two mythological figural themes found on some examples of R. S. Prussia. These two decorations were based on paintings by the French portrait painter, Nattier (1685 – 1766). Nattier was also a painter at the court of Louis XV. "Madame Adelaide as Diana" and "Madame Henriette as Flora" are two of his popular works.

Diana, according to mythology, was one of the goddesses of Olympus. Her portrayal as the huntress was only one of the several legends identified with her. As the huntress, she was often shown with a bow, a quiver of arrows, hounds, or deer. She was also sometimes pictured resting after the hunt. That is the particular type of scene found on R. S. Prussia china.

Flora was the Italian goddess of flowers and symbol of spring. She is usually portrayed as a woman with flowers. The china transfer shows a lady reclining, holding a floral garland. Multi-colored flowers are in the foreground. Collectors sometimes refer to this figure as the Reclining Lady.

Most of the china decorated with Diana or Flora has a Royal Vienna mark or is not marked. Some pieces have both the Royal Vienna mark and the R. S. Prussia mark, and a few have only the R. S. Prussia mark, but they are in the minority. In the Fourth Series, I discuss the Royal Vienna mark and show examples which have only the Royal Vienna mark. A number of pieces are shown which are decorated with Flora or Diana; see that edition for elaboration on the subject. The pieces shown here are marked unless noted otherwise.

Diana and Flora decorations are popular among collectors, regardless of whether the china is marked or unmarked. Like the Four Seasons or the Melon Eaters and Dice Throwers, Diana and Flora transfers were often used together. One figure might decorate one side of a vase, and the other the reverse side. Both figures can be found as medallion or cameo decoration on bowls, trays, or plates. They are usually on very decorative pieces which were clearly designed to be displayed. Values are generally less for these decorations than for the Four Seasons and other portraits such as Lebrun.

Plate 719. *Cake Plate, 10½"d, Mold 343; Diana the Huntress in center of plate with Cupids in reserves on border; iridescent Tiffany finish around border; gold trim. $600.00 – 800.00.*

Plate 720. *Ewer, 7¼"h, 5½"w, Mold 959; Diana the Huntress on front with Flora on reverse; cobalt blue finish; gold trim; unmarked. $1,200.00 – 1,400.00.*

Plate 721. *Tankard, 12"h, Mold 640; Diana the Huntress; iridescent Tiffany finish; RSP mark with the Royal Vienna Mark. $700.00 – 900.00.*

Plate 722. *Bowl, 10½"d, Mold 82, Point and Clover Mold; Flora decorates the center with scenes from Victorian Vignettes decorating the cameos within the dome shapes on the border; gold stencilled work and gold trim. $1,400.00 – 1,600.00.*

Plate 723. *Celery Dish, 14"l, 7"w, Mold 14, Medallion Mold; FD36, Reflecting Poppies and Daisies decorate center with Diana and Flora on border medallions. $500.00 – 600.00.*

Plate 724. *Vase, 11"h, Mold 931; Flora on front with Cherubs (not shown) on reverse; Tiffany finish; RSP mark with the Royal Vienna Mark. $1,200.00 – 1,400.00.*

Plate 725. *Vase, 9¼"h, Mold 945; Flora in a reserve on front with Diana on reverse side (not shown); cobalt blue finish above and below the white center with portrait; gold stencilled designs highlight the dark finish. $1,000.00 – 1,200.00.*

Plate 726. *Ewer, 7¼"h, Mold 959; Flora on the reverse side of Ewer shown in Plate 720 with Diana on the front; unmarked. $1,200.00 – 1,400.00.*

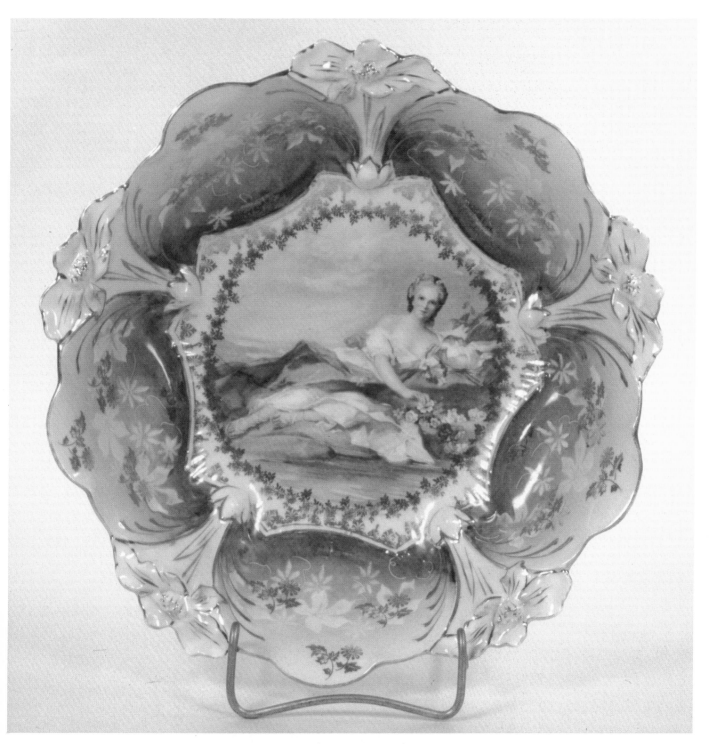

Plate 727. *Bowl, 10"d, Mold 29, Lily Mold; Flora decorates the center; tinted blue finish around outer border; gold stencilled designs and gold trim; unmarked. $800.00 – 1,000.00.*

Plate 728. Bowl, 10½"d, Mold 10i, Leaf Mold variation; Flora portrait; an aqua-green finish around portrait highlights figure; unmarked. $800.00 – 1,000.00.

Plate 729. Bowl, 10½"d, Mold 354; Flora surrounded by a dark green border and gold stencilled designs; a gold stippled outer border is accented by a dark green trim; unmarked. $900.00 – 1,100.00.

Four Charmers, Napoleon, Nightwatch Figures, Peace Bringing Plenty, The Cage, and Victorian Vignettes (Plates 730 – 742)

In this section some figures and portraits are shown which may infrequently be found on R. S. Prussia china. A few seem to be more prevalent than others. Also some of these decorations can be found with other R. S. marks. A few with R. S. Prussia marks are included here so that new collectors will be aware of these particular decorations. Scarce does not necessarily mean rare, and thus values for some of these scarce decorations are not in the same high ranges as for animal themes, for example.

The Four Charmers, however, are considered rare. Victorian women are shown in four poses: one holding a letter; one with a bowl of apples; one holding her hands to her head; and one wearing a cape in a winter scene. Only the Girl with Letter is shown here. See Barlock, Plate 9, for examples of the other three.

Napoleon and Josephine in portrait form are found on china with different R. S. marks as well as with E. S. marks. The Nightwatch Figures are based on the famous Rembrandt painting. This decoration is found with the R. S. Suhl and R. S. Poland marks as well as the R. S. Prussia mark.

Peace Bringing Plenty is a transfer decoration found on some R. S. marked china, including R. S. Prus-sia, R. S. Germany, and R. S. Tillowitz. This decoration is based on the painting "La Paix Qui Ramené L'Abondance" by Madame Lebrun. Peace is usually portrayed by a dove and less frequently by a woman, as in Lebrun's painting. In the decoration, Peace is a fair-haired maiden bringing a basket of fruit to a dark-haired maiden.

Another scarce figural scene is based on "The Cage," a painting by Françoise Boucher (1703 – 1770), court painter to King Louis XV. Boucher was noted for romantic subjects as well as landscapes, portraits, and mythological scenes. The transfer decoration is a romantic theme featuring a boy and a girl sitting in a wooded area with flowers and a bird cage in the foreground.

A number of other figural decorations are grouped under the name of Victorian Vignettes. Pastoral settings and figures in Victorian dress show couples in several courting scenes. I have not included the set of Lady figural decorations illustrating a Lady Watering Flowers, a Lady Feeding Chickens, a Lady with a Fan, and a Lady with a Dog. Because such decorations are usually unmarked, R. S. Steeple marked, or Royal Vienna marked, they have been included in the Fourth Series.

Plate 730. *Plate, 8½"d, Mold 306; Girl with Letter, one of the Four Charmers, satin finish. $2,200.00 – 2,400.00.*

Plate 731. *Syrup Pitcher, 6"h, and Underplate, 6"d, Mold 631, Medallion Mold; cameo portrait of Napoleon on gold tapestry background; FD90, sitting basket, below portrait; red finish on top borders and lid. $500.00 – 600.00 set.*

Plate 732. *Reverse side of Syrup Pitcher with cameo portrait of Josephine.*

Plate 733. Vase, 4½"h, salesman's sample, Mold 909; Figures from the Nightwatch Scene; dark green finish. $600.00 – 800.00.

Plate 734. Vase, 6"h, Mold 913; Peace Bringing Plenty. $600.00 – 800.00.

Plate 735. Cake Plate, 10"d, Mold 341; The Cage figural scenic decor; iridescent dark rose-colored inner border and outer trim. $1,000.00 – 1,200.00.

Plate 736. Vase, 6"h, Mold 928; The Cage (a reverse position of figures in this version of the decoration). $600.00 – 800.00.

Plate 737. Covered Urn, 11"h, Mold 962; The Cage; deep rose finish overlaid with gold stencilled designs. $1,800.00 – 2,000.00.

Plate 738. Cake Plate, 9"d, Mold 182; Victorian Vignette: couple seated in forest decorates center with other couples in reserves around border. $250.00 – 300.00.

Plate 740. Vase, 8¾"h, Mold 911; Victorian Vignette: couple with woman knitting and sheep in the background. $500.00 – 600.00.

Plate 739. Vase, 4½"h, salesman's sample, Mold 909; Victorian Vignette: courting scene on yellow to brown background. $250.00 – 300.00.

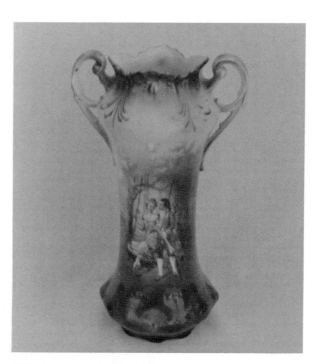

Plate 741. Vase, 7¼"h, Mold 912; Victorian Vignette: couple with woman in a swing. $400.00 – 500.00.

Plate 742. Vase, 9"h, Mold 918; Victorian Vignette: another version of a couple with the woman in a swing and the man behind her. $500.00 – 600.00.

Scenic Decorations
(Plates 743 – 756)

The Peary Arctic Expedition (1909) is featured on R. S. Prussia china to commemorate that historic event. One scene features warmly dressed figures with an igloo and the American Flag. Another shows a figure on skis with huskies confronting a polar bear with a snow and ice background. These decorations are very rare.

A few other scenic designs are not frequently found, but they are not considered rare like the Admiral Peary scenes. Values are considerably less for the following scarce scenic decorations: Masted Ships or Schooners in two different versions; another Sheep-herder design; scenes of a Country House and Lake; and a Farm Scene. Some of these scenes may be on china with other R. S. marks.

Three Scenes refer to pieces decorated with three different transfers. The white swans, turkeys, swallows, pheasant, and barnyard animals can be found as decoration transfers on individual pieces. Due to the popularity of those birds as a single decoration, collectors especially like items which show all three. Pieces with Three Scenes are considered rare and values are high.

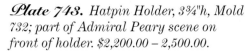

Plate 743. *Hatpin Holder, 3¾"h, Mold 732; part of Admiral Peary scene on front of holder. $2,200.00 – 2,500.00.*

Plate 744. *Lemonade Pitcher, 6½"h, Mold 656, companion to Mold 732; Admiral Peary with American flag. $6,500.00 – 7,500.00.*

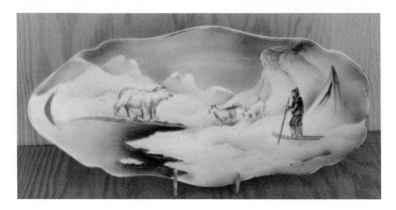

Plate 745. *Celery Dish, 11½"l, Mold 349; Admiral Peary Arctic scene, "Midst Snow and Ice" printed in lower right hand corner. $5,000.00 – 6,000.00.*

Plate 746. Cake Set: Cake Plate, 11"d, six Individual Plates, 6"d, Mold 207; Masted Ship decor with a pearl luster finish. Serving Plate, $1,200.00 – 1,400.00; Individual Plates, $100.00 – 150.00 each.

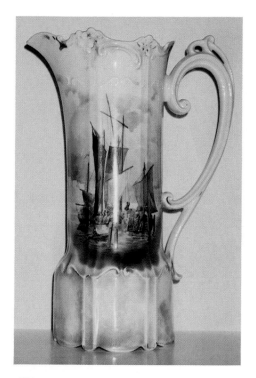

Plate 747. Tankard, 11½"h, Mold 537; Masted Schooner on a white background. $1,600.00 – 1,800.00.

Plate 748. *Oval Bowl, 13"l, 9"w, Mold 207; a second Masted Ship decoration, differentiated from the above by the leaning mast. $1,400.00 – 1,600.00.*

Plate 749. *Chocolate Pot, Mold 642, companion to Mold 207; Masted Schooner with leaning mast on rust to cream background. $1,400.00 – 1,600.00.*

Plate 750. *Vase, 11"h, Mold 906; a second Sheepherder scene with white birch trees in the foreground. $1,000.00 – 1,200.00.*

Plate 751. Plate, 10"d, Mold 426a; Country House and Lake with figures on the bank. $800.00 – 1,000.00.

Plate 752. Bowl, 10½"d, Mold 253; Farm Scene with a house in the background and a farmer in the foreground. $800.00 – 1,000.00.

Plate 753. Plate, 6"d, Mold 304; three scenes: Swallows, Pheasant, and Swan; gold trim; unmarked. $600.00 – 800.00.

Plate 754. *Plate 8½"d, Mold 304; three scenes: Turkeys, Swans, and Swallows. $2,500.00 – 3,000.00.*

Plate 755. *Tankard, 13"h, Mold 582; three scenes: Swans, Ducks, and Swallows. $6,000.00 – 7,000.00.*

Plate 756. *Celery Dish, 12½"l, Mold 304; three scenes: Barnyard Animals, Swans, and Swallows. $3,000.00 – 3,500.00.*

Chapter 7

Reproductions

Identifying Fakes and Repairs

Some examples of the faked R.S. Prussia mark and misleading "R.S." marks which were shown in my earlier books are reprinted here. Some other new versions of the fake decal RSP mark are also included as well as a new R.S. Suhl fake mark. While the fake RSP wreath marks have looked relatively authentic, the fake RS Suhl mark does not. It is too large, and the letter "l" in Suhl is capitalized (L). That letter in the authentic mark is in the lower case.

Antique malls, shops, and flea markets carry many of these new items. The same lines of pieces and patterns which were being made in the early 1980s are still being made. Sometimes the marks on the pieces are the fake RSP mark or the misleading R.S. Wreath marks. But many of those items now have the fake R.S. Suhl mark. The same pieces can also be found with fake Limoges and Nippon marks. There is also another mark appearing on similar items. This mark is sometimes referred to as "Crown Prussia." It consists of a crown with a "P" beneath the crown.

While all of the contemporary china is certainly not equal in quality to Schlegelmilch china, collectors and dealers continue to be "taken" by these modern pieces. Usually the price can be the clue to whether or not the item is genuine. Beware of low prices. When these pieces are offered for sale in most retail outlets, the prices are not exorbitant, but they are still somewhat higher than what the importer sells them for. The bell shown in the following photographs was priced at $6.00 at one outlet, while down the road, another was selling it for $14.00.

Higher prices on these reproductions are often found at antique shows. Chocolate sets like those shown here have been seen with price tags of $200.00. A fair price for such modern pieces would be less than $40.00.

The importers continue to place gold stick-on labels on the pieces. These stickers may carry the name of the importer as well as the notation of "Made in Japan." Collectors who purchase these items with the stickers still on them really have no one but themselves to blame for buying such reproductions. The stickers, of course, are easily removed, and thus unscrupulous dealers simply take them off and price according to "what the market will bear." (Isn't it amazing how easily these stickers can be removed. Most stickers on their modern goods are glued on so well that one must scrub them off or even resort to using some form of chemical remover!)

The reproductions which were shown in the First Series have been reprinted here. While some of these are still being made, new patterns have also been introduced. Examples of four of the new designs are shown along with one picture of the pattern which has the "Crown Prussia" mark. No prices are listed in the Price Guide for these reproductions. Dealers should purchase catalogs from wholesale houses to keep abreast of new items and patterns of modern reproductions. Collectors should routinely be alert to large displays of china offered for sale which have floral, figural, or portrait decorations with RSP or RS Suhl marks. Examine marks and china carefully and ask the dealer for a money back guarantee if the item turns out to be a modern reproduction.

Repaired porcelain may cause almost as much concern for collectors as the fake marks and modern reproductions. I discussed this topic in the first edition. Businesses have been specializing in repairing R.S. Prussia for many years. It is inevitable that such pieces eventually find their way on the market. Some collectors desire to have a piece repaired when it becomes damaged. There is nothing wrong with that. The problem, of course, occurs when such pieces are later sold without the buyer being aware that a repair has been made.

There is certainly no rule of thumb for knowing whether or not a piece of china has been repaired. Professional china restorers are quite skillful. Some are less adept than others, however. Pieces may "fall apart," or handles, feet, and finials may come off pieces which have been improperly or hastily repaired. Collectors should always examine china carefully in a good, natural light. The eyes can deceive, and thus the object should be examined by going over the surface by hand as well. See that lids really fit and that all handles and feet match. Check for roughness or unevenness of body texture. Again, the best advice is to purchase from reputable dealers who stand behind their merchandise.

Repaired china should not be priced the same as china in good condition. R.S. Prussia prices, however, are often quite similar for repaired pieces and those in good condition. This is not likely to change until collectors begin to demand that not only are repairs indicated by sellers, but also that repaired pieces' prices are proportionately discounted according to the amount of damage.

Fake R.S. Prussia Mark 1.

Fake R.S. Prussia Mark 2.

Fake R.S. Prussia Mark 3.

Fake R.S. Mark 4, red wreath and star with initials.

Fake R.S. Prussia Mark 5, red wreath and star with initials.

Misleading Wreath Mark in green, Mark 6.

R1. *Jewel Box, 10"l, 8"w; "signed" Boucher, Fake Mark 1, 5, or Fake R.S. Suhl mark. Similar boxes with other designs are also made.*

R2. *Egg Box, 5½"l; "signed" Boucher; Misleading Wreath Mark 6.*

R3. *Plate, 7"d; "signed" Boucher; Fake Mark 4.*

R4. *Bell, 5¼"h; same pastoral scene as preceding three photos. This example does not have a "signature"; Fake Mark 4.*

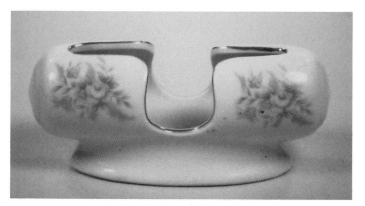

R5. Card Holder, 4½"l; pink rose pattern; Fake Mark 3.

R7. Cracker Jar, 8"h; yellow rose pattern; Fake Mark 5.

R6. Pitcher, 12"h; roses with cobalt blue finish; Fake Mark 2.

R9. Hatpin Holder, 5½"h; pink rose pattern on light blue back-ground; Fake Mark 4.

R8. Left-Handed Mustache Cup, 3" x 3¾", and Saucer, 7"d; yellow rose pattern; Fake Mark 5.

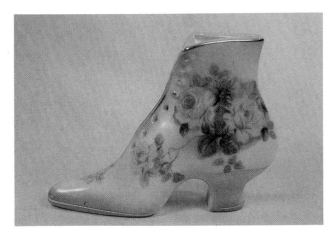

R11. *Shoe with high top; pink rose pattern; Fake Mark 4.*

R12. *Saucer, 5½"d; pink rose pattern; Fake Mark 4.*

R10. *Ewer, 5"h (like RSP Mold 640); pink rose pattern on light blue and pink background; Fake Mark 4.*

R13. *Candy Dish, 8"l x 6"w (like RSP Mold 528 in Plate 631); multicolored roses; Misleading Wreath Mark 6.*

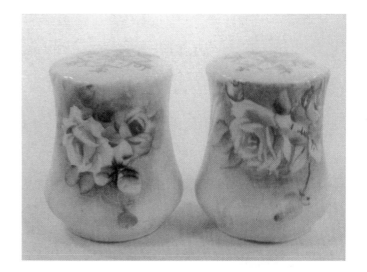

R14. Salt and Pepper Shakers, 2½"h; pink roses; Fake Mark 2.

R15. Mustache Cup, 3½"h; pink roses, wide gold border; Fake Mark 2.

R16. Cracker Jar, 7"h; pink rose spray, gold trim; Fake Mark 2.

R17. Cracker Jar, 5"h, no handles; pink roses; Fake Mark 2.

R18. Bowl, 16"d; Pitcher, 11½"h; transfer portrait of Countess Potocka with "Monreau" as signature on lower right side of bust. This is not an RSP transfer. Pieces have Fake Mark 1.

Fake R.S. Suhl Mark,
spelled "SuhL."

R19. Coffee Set: Pot, Covered Sugar Bowl, Creamer, and Cup and Saucer; pink rose pattern on tinted blue and pink background; Fake R.S. Suhl Mark.

R20. *Chocolate Set: Pot and Mugs; light pink poppies in a stylized design; Fake R.S. Suhl Mark.*

R21. *Footed Bowl, 13"l, 6⅛"h, pierced work around border; cluster of pink roses with beige tinted borders and gold trim; Fake R.S. Suhl Mark.*

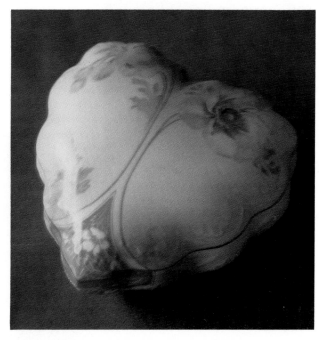

R22. *Heart-shaped Box, 5" x 5"; light pink poppies in a stylized design; Fake R.S. Suhl Mark.*

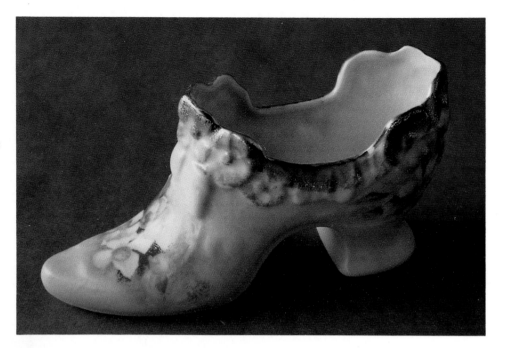

R23. *Shoe, 6½"l; two white dogwood blossoms with a pink flower; blue border with gold spattered work; Fake R.S. Suhl Mark.*

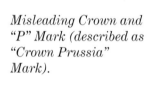

Misleading Crown and "P" Mark (described as "Crown Prussia" Mark).

R24. *Muffineer, 4½"h; pale pink and lavender roses; Fake R.S. Suhl Mark.*

R25. *Rectangular Box with pierced opening; Vase; Shell-shaped Dish; yellow rose pattern on tinted blue background; Misleading Crown and "P" Mark.*

Bibliography

Adressbuch der Keram-Industrie. Coburg: Müller & Schmidt, 1893, 1910, 1913, 1930, 1932, 1934, 1937, 1941, 1949.

Ananoff, Alexandre. *L'oeuvre Dessiné de Francois Boucher.* Paris: F. De Nobele, Librarie, 1966.

Barber, Edwin Atlee. *The Ceramic Collectors' Glossary.* New York: Da Capo Press, 1967.

Barlock, George E. and Eileen. *The Treasures of R.S. Prussia.* 1976.

Bartran, Margaret. *A Guide to Color Reproductions.* Second edition. Metuchen, NJ: The Scarecrow Press, Inc., 1971.

Bearne, Mrs. *A Court Painter and His Circle, Francois Boucher.* London: Adelphi Terrace, 1913.

Benson, E.F. *The White Eagle of Poland.* New York: George H. Doran Company, n.d.

Boger, Louise Ade. *The Dictionary of World Pottery and Porcelain.* New York: Charles Scribner's Sons, 1971.

Buell, Raymond Leslie. *Poland: Key to Europe.* London: Jonathan Cape, 1939.

Calvert, Albert F. (ed.). *Murillo: The Spanish Series.* London: John Lane, The Bodley Head Gallery, 1907.

Capers, R. H. *Discussions with Gerhard Soppa,* November 26 and 27, 1991.

———. "R.S. Made in (German) Poland" *Mark, R. S. Prussia* (Number 16, February, 1992): 8-10.

———. *Capers' Notes on the Marks of Prussia.* El Paso, IL: Alphabet Printing, Inc., 1996.

Castries, Duc de. *Madame Récamier.* Hachette, 1971.

Catalogue of Reproductions of Paintings Prior to 1860. Paris: UNESCO, 1972.

Chaffers, William. *Handbook of Marks and Monograms on Pottery and Porcelain.* Revised edition. London: William Reeves, 1968.

———. *Marks & Monograms on Pottery and Porcelain.* Vol. 1, 15th Revised edition. London: William Reeves, 1965.

Chróscicki, Leon. *Porcelana – Znaki Wytworni Europejskich.* Warszawa: Wybawnictwo Artystyczno-Graficzne, 1974.

Cox, W. E. *The Book of Pottery and Porcelain.* Vol. 1. New York: L. Lee Shepard Co., Inc., 1944.

Cushion, J. P. *Pocket Book of German Ceramic Marks and Those of Other Central European Countries.* London: Faber and Faber, 1961.

Cushion, J.P. (in collaboration with W.B. Honey). *Handbook of Pottery and Porcelain Marks.* London: Faber & Faber, 1956.

Danckert, Ludwig. *Hanbuch des Europäischen Porzellans.* Munich: Prestel Verlag, 1954, 1967, 1978, 1984, 1992.

Day, William E. *Blue Book of Art Values.* Third edition, Paducah, KY: Collector Books, 1979.

Dyboski, Roman. *Outlines of Polish History.* London: George Allen & Unwin, Ltd. Revised edition, 1931.

Encyclopedia Britannica. Vol 18. Chicago: William Benton, 1970.

Fayard Artheme (ed.) *Souvenirs De Mme. Louise Elsabeth Vigee-LeBrun.* Paris: F. Funch-Bretana.

Gaston, Mary Frank. *The Collector's Encyclopedia of Limoges Porcelain.* Paducah, KY: Collector Books, 1980.

———. *The Collector's Encyclopedia of R.S. Prussia.* Paducah KY: Collector Books, 1982.

———. "Rare R. S. (Schlegelmilch) Marks." *Schroeder's Insider,* December, 1983.

———. "More Schlegelmilch Marks!" *Schroeder's Insider,* October, 1984.

———. *The Collector's Encyclopedia of R.S. Prussia,* Second Series. Paducah, KY: Collector Books, 1986.

———. "Schlegelmilch China: Ambiguous, Scarce, and New Marks." Presentation at the annual meeting of the International Association of R. S. Prussia Collectors, Inc., August, 1991.

———. *The Collector's Encyclopedia of R.S. Prussia,* Third Series. Paducah, KY: Collector Books, 1994.

———. *The Collector's Encyclopedia of R.S. Prussia,* Fourth Series. Paducah, KY: Collector Books, 1995.

Graul, Richard and Albrecht Kurzwelly. *Alt Thuringer Porzellan,* 1909.

Haggar, Reginald G. *The Concise Encyclopedia of Continental Pottery and Porcelain.* New York: Hawthorne Books, Inc. 1960.

Hall, James. *Dictionary of Subjects and Symbols in Art.* Revised edition. New York: Harper & Row, 1979.

Hammon, Dorothy. *Confusing Collectibles.* Des Moines, Iowa: Wallace Homestead, 1969.

Hartwich, Bernd. *The History of the Suhl Porcelain Factories 1861 – 1937.* Tasked by the Technical School for Museum Caretakers. Leipzeig & Weapons Museum, Suhl, Germany, 1984. (Translation by R.H. Capers.)

Hayden, C. Chumley. *Why R.S.Prussia?* Springfield, OR: C. Chumley Hayden, 1970.

Heimatkalender des Kreifes Falkenberg (Hometown Almanac for the County of Falkenberg), 1927. (Translation by R.H. Capers.)

Honey, W.B. *German Porcelain.* London: Faber and Faber, 1947.

Hymanson, Albert M. *A Dictionary of Universal Biography of all Ages and of all People.* Second edition. New York: E.P. Dutton & Co., Inc. 1951.

"Wilhelm Kahlert." Obituary in *Grottkain-Falkenberger Heimatblat,* Nr. 24, 1967. (Translation by R.H. Capers.)

Klingenbrunn, Marietta. *Deutsche Porzellanmarken von 1708 bis beute.* Augsburg, Germany: Battenburg Verlag, 1990.

Kovel, Ralph and Terry. *Kovel's New Dictionary of*

Marks. New York: Crown Publications, Inc., 1986.

Kraemer, Ekkehard. *Sächsisch-thüringischès Manufakturporzellan*, 1985.

LaRousse Encyclopedia of World Geography. New York: Odyssey Press. Adapted from Geographie Universelle Larousse, Western Publishing Co., 1965.

Lehner, Lois. *Complete Book of American Kitchen and Dinnerware.* Des Moines: Wallace-Homestead, 1980.

———. *Lehner's Encyclopedia of U.S. Marks on Pottery, Porcelain & Clay.* Paducah, KY: Collector Books, 1988.

Lehr, Margaret Marshall and Margaret Pattie Follet. *A Scrapbook About Old China.* Moorhead, MN: Follett Studios, 1964.

Leistikow-Duchardt, Annelore. *Die Entwicklung eines neuen Stiles im Porzellan.* Heidelberg: Carl Winter Universitatsverlag, 1957.

Lewis, C.T. Courtney. *The Picture Printer of the Nineteenth Century: George Baxter.* London: Sampson Law, Marsten & Co., Ltd. 1911.

"A Life's Romance." *The Aldine.* January, 1873.

Lucas, E.V. *Chardin and Vigee-Lebrun.* London: Methuen & Co., Ltd., n.d.

McCaslin, Mary. "A Visit to Tillowitz, Poland – A Lot of Surprises." *R.S. Prussia* (Number 18, July 1992): 5-7.

McCaslin, Mary and Robert. "R.S. Prussia Club Restores Schlegelmilch Grave Site." *Antique Week* (July 27, 1992): 12 and 23.

McCaslin, Robert. "Answers From the Past." *R.S. Prussia* (Number 18, July 1992): 8.

Marple, Lee. "Hidden Images." Presentation at the annual meeting of the International Association of R.S. Prussia Collectors, Inc., August 1991.

Meyers Grosses Konversations-Lexikon. Sixth edition. Vol 17. Leipzig and Vienna: Biographisches Institu, 1907.

Mountfield, David. *The Antique Collectors' Illustrated Dictionary.* London, Hamlyn, 1974.

Muehsam, Gerd (ed.). *French Painters and Paintings from the Fourteenth Century to Post Impressionism.* New York: Fredrich Ungar Publishing Co., 1970.

Norman, Colleen and Rose Greider. "Identification of Unmarked Pieces." Presentation at the annual meeting of the International Association of R.S. Prussia Collectors, Inc., August, 1991.

Norman, Geraldine. *Nineteenth-Century Painters and Painting: A Dictionary.* Thames and Hudson, 1977.

Pattloch, Franz. *"Erinnerung an Tillowitz/Oberichelian"* [Memories of Tillowitz, Upper Silesia.] No date or source for periodical; post World War II refugee publication. (Translated by R.H. Capers).

Penkala, Maria. *European Porcelain: A Handbook for the Collector.* Second edition. Rutland, VT: Charles E. Tuttle, 1968.

Poche, Emanuel. *Porcelain Marks of the World.* New York: Arco Publishing Co., Inc., 1974.

Porcelit Tulowicki [Stoneware from Tulowice]. Monograph of the "Tillowice" Porcelit Plant as presented by the Exhibition Office, Opole, June-July 1984. (Translated by Roman Zawada.)

"Porzellan kommt aus OS" [Porcelain Comes out of Upper Silesia]. *Breslauer Neweste Nachrichten* (April 10, 1938). (Translated by R.H. Capers.)

Röntgen, Robert E. *Marks on German, Bohemian and Austrian Porcelain: 1710 to the Present.* Exton, PA: Schiffer Publishing Co., 1981.

Rose, William John. *The Drama of Upper Silesia.* Brattleboro, VT: Stephen Daye Press, 1935.

Schlegelmilch, Clifford J. *Handbook of Erdmann and Reinhold Schlegelmilch, Prussia-Germany and Oscar Schlegelmilch, Germany.* Third edition, 1973.

Sorenson, Don C. *My Collection R.S. Prussia*, 1979.

Stryienski, Casimir (ed.) *Memoirs of the Countess Potocka.* New York: Doubleday & McClure Co., 1901.

Terrell, George W., Jr. *Collecting R.S. Prussia: Identification and Values:* Florence, AL: Books Americana, 1982.

Thalheim, Karl G. and A. Hillen Ziegfeld (eds.) *Der deutsche Osten. Seine Geschichte, sein Wesen und seine Aufgabe.* Berlin: Propylaen, 1936.

The Antique Trader Price Guide to Antiques. Dubuque, IA: Babka Publishing Company, Inc., Summer 1979, Volume X., No. 2, Issue No. 32.

The Ceramist. Vol. 3 (Winter Quarter), 1923.

The International Geographic Encyclopedia and Atlas. Boston: Houghton Mifflin Company, 1979.

The World Book Atlas. Field Enterprises Education Corporation, 1973.

Thorne, J.O. (ed.). *Chambers Biographical Dictionary.* Revised edition. New York: St. Martin's Press, 1969.

Treharne, R.F. and Harold Fullard (eds.). *Muir's Historical Atlas Medieval and Modern.* Tenth edition. New York: Barnes and Noble, Inc., 1964.

Wandycz, Piotr S. *The Lands of Paritioned Poland, 1795 – 1918.* Seattle: University of Washington Press, 1923.

Warzecha, Richard. "Ein Besuch in der Tillowitzer Porzellanfabrik" [A Visit to the Tillowitz Porcelain Factory], circa 1953. Publication source unknown. (Translated by R.H. Capers.)

Webster's Biographical Dictionary. Springfield, MA: G. and C. Merriam Company, 1976.

Webster's New Geographical Dictionary. Springfield, MA; G. and C. Merriam Company, 1972.

Weis, Gustav. *Ullstein Porzellanbuch.* Frankfurt, Berlin, Wein: Verlag Ullstein Gimblt, 1975. First edition, 1964.

Wenke, George "Tillowitzer Porzellaneschichte." *Unser Oberschlesien* (August 22, 1984). (Translated by R.H. Capers.)

Zühlsdorff, Dieter. *Marken Exikon – Porzellan und Keramik Report 1885 – 1935.* Stuttgart: Arnoldsche, 1988.

Appendices
R.S. Prussia Mold Identification Numbers and Popular Names

Please note the examples of RSP Molds shown in this chart refer to Plates in the Third Series.
RSP molds in this current edition are dispersed and not grouped as in Books 1, 2, and 3.

Category 1 - Flat or Round Objects

Mold Numbers	Plate Numbers	Type of Mold	General Characteristics
1-50	1-81	Popular Named Molds (Iris, etc.)	A particular feature in the body or the border of the mold suggests an obvious mold name.
51-75	82-86	Floral Border Molds	The border of the mold is composed of floral designs usually separated by other shapes such as scallops or points. The floral designs are not always easy to see at first glance.
76-150	87-141	Unusual Body Shape	The body of the mold is composed of blown out sections usually in the form of dome or star shapes.
151-180	142-150	Pointed Border Molds	The overall border design is pointed. There may be notched indentations between the points. Such molds must be easily distinguishable from scalloped molds and have no rounded sides.
181-200	151-155	Rounded Scalloped Border	Border has rounded scallop sections of equal size. The sections may be beaded or fluted.
201-250	156-170	Semi-round Scalloped Border	The scallop sections are not perfectly round. There may be a slight indentation or some other configuration between the scallops. The edges of the scallops can be smooth, beaded, or fluted.
251-275	171-186	Crimped Scalloped Border	Scallop sections are pinched or indented.
276-299	187-192	Wavy Scalloped Border	The scallop sections resemble a wavy line with a slight rounded center and shallow indentations on each side. The wavy sections may be separated by other small configurations such as scroll designs or points.
300-325	193-209	Elongated Scalloped Border	The scallop sections are long rather than round. The center of the section has either a slight indentation or a sharp rounded point. The elongated scallops may be separated by other small configurations.
326-400	210-229	Irregular Scalloped Borders	Borders are composed or more than one of the above kind of scallops or some other configuration such as a point or scroll design. These molds are usually quite elaborate.
401-425	230-232	Scrolled Borders	Border is composed of ornate, curving scallop designs not only on the border but extending into the body of the object.
426-450	233-244	Smooth Borders	Border is completely smooth. The overall shape of the object may vary: round, oval, or rectangular.

Category 2 - Vertical or Tall Objects

Mold Numbers	Plate Numbers	Type of Mold	General Characteristics
451-500	245-262; 323	Smooth Bases	Base of object is perfectly level or flat on the bottom.
501-575	263-322; 324-363	Flat Scalloped Base	The border of the base of the object is scalloped, but there is no elevation.
576-600	364-375	Elevated Scalloped Base	The base of the object has a scallop border composed of equal or varied sized scallops. Indentations between the scallops elevate the object slightly.
601-625	376-391	Pedestal Foot	Objects may have a long or a short pedestal base. Long pedestals have a stem section between the base and body; short pedestals have no stem section. The bases of the pedestals may be round, square, smooth, or scalloped.
626-700	392-472	Molded Feet	Feet for the object are shaped as part of the body mold.
701-725	473-487	Applied Feet	Definite feet are applied to the base of the object.

Category 3 - Accessory Items

Mold Numbers	Plate Numbers	Type of Mold
726-775	488-489	Hatpin Holders
776-800	490-493	Muffineers/Talcum Shakers
801-825	494-504	Hair Receivers
826-850	505-516	Boxes: Match, Pin, Powder
851-855	517	Candle Holders
856-860		Letter Holders

Category 4 - Ferners and Vases

Mold Numbers	Plate Numbers	Type of Mold
876-899	518-522	Ferners
900-975	524-583	Vases/Ewers/Urns

Mold Numbers and Popular Names

(Gaston Mold Numbers may be found variously in this edition
or the First, Second, or Third Series)

Gaston Mold Number	Popular Name	Gaston Mold Number	Popular Name
1,583	Acorn	502	Morning Glory
632	Ball Foot		Nut (see Acorn)
32, 32a, 32b	Berry	586	Open Base
33	Bleeding Heart	528, also 802	Pagoda
504, 813	Bow Tie	15	Pentagon
	Cabbage (see Lettuce)	36, 649; also 255, 256	Pie Crust
28, 28a, 519, 520,	Carnation or Poppy	951; also 952	Pillow
526; also 55, 402		16, 465, 658, 836	Plume
	Circle (see Medallion)	81, 82, 611, 643	Point and Clover
261	Corduroy	91	Point and Flower
	Daisy (see Lily)	92	Popcorn
548	Daisy and Scroll	17	Puff
841	Egg Basket or Carton	657	Raspberry
601	Egg on Pedestal	451, 472, 545, 634	Reversed Swirl
	Feather (see Plume)	18, 522, 645, 817, 835,	Ribbon and Jewel
207, 642	Flame and Jewel	932, 936, 963; also 333	
646	Fleur and Jewel	259, 536, 815	Ripple
9, 609, 929; also 214	Fleur-de-lis	300	Rope Edge
527	Flower Form		Ruffle (see Stippled
2, 2a, 2b, 2c	Grape		Floral)
3	Heart	98	Sawtooth
577	Hexagon	508, 540, 540a, 729	Scallop
34	Honey Comb	278, 501	Scallop and Fan
7, 8, 466, 641, 806	Icicle	19	Sea Creature
25, 25a, 25b, 518, 628	Iris	20	Shell
257	Ivy and Icicle	37, 37a	Shield
	Jewel (see Ribbon and	78	Six Medallion
	Jewel)	21	Spoonholder
10, 10a through 10i	Leaf	22	Square and Jewel
627, 627a, 627b	Leaf Base	23, 525, 826	Stippled Floral
12, 12a, 12b	Lettuce	38, 482	Strawberry
29, 30, 517	Lily	31, 463, 553, 626	Sunflower
473	Lily of the Valley	155, 582, 633	Swag and Tassel
53, 53a	Lily Pad	39	Tear Drop
35, 35a, 35b	Locket	40, 811, 839	Tulip and Ribbon
13	Maize	90	Violet
14, 14a, 631	Medallion	24	Wheat Fleur-de-lis

R.S. Prussia Floral Identification Chart

One hundred floral transfers found on R.S. Prussia marked china have been assigned a Floral Identification number for this edition. The numbers include some of the popular named floral patterns such as "Reflecting Water Lilies," "Roses and Snowballs," "Hanging Basket," and so forth. These various popular named patterns are described by number and name in the captions of the photographs. The other floral patterns are described by number with a brief description of the design. The description is not always included in the caption, however. Readers may refer to this index to find the description of the numbered pattern if necessary. A list of the RSP Floral Identification numbers (FD#) and their descriptions are provided here. Examples of those specific floral transfers shown in the photographs are listed by plate number. A notation of G3 indicates that the example is in only the Third Series and not in this edition.

To describe the floral patterns, I have used only the chief characteristics of the particular design. The number generally refers to the primary pattern on the piece. Sometimes two floral transfers may be found on the same piece, and, thus, the example will have more than one FD#. The large center floral decorations usually do have other floral designs scattered randomly around the inner and outer borders. These may differ from the central pattern, but such designs are not identified by FD# unless the design is one of the 100 transfers used for this identification system.

I also have not assigned numbers to most of the small floral patterns such as small garlands, single blooms, and small clusters of flowers. The numbers are basically restricted to the larger patterns. Some of the names used to describe the floral designs may differ among collectors from those I use here. Some of the flowers are not easily distinguishable. Roses may look like poppies and vice versa. Lilacs, pansies, clematis, and so forth are other floral shapes which might be confusing. The colors may vary for the patterns, either by design, or through the lighting used for the photograph. Pink, yellow, white, and orange as well as other colors may appear either darker or lighter than they actually are. Thus, a red may appear as dark pink, or a pale yellow may seem to be white. The configuration of the floral design is more important in determining a specific pattern than the color of the flowers.

The floral patterns found on R.S. Prussia china appear to be endless, but after studying hundreds of examples, it is evident that the number of primary designs is probably in the low hundreds rather than thousands. The placement of the embellishments around the central patterns makes it appear as though there are more patterns than there actually are. The 100 designs identified here are certainly not all of the primary floral patterns. From the photographs, which are from a random sample, it is apparent that many pieces and molds have the same floral pattern. A few of the FD numbers are listed with an "a" or "b." These letters indicate that the pattern is either similar to the one with the whole number, or that it is a part of that transfer.

RSP FD#	Description of Pattern	Examples
1	three full light pink roses and one dark pink rose	244-251
2	multi-colored roses with a white rose on a hairpin bent stem	252-266
3	one red rose and one white rose	267-299
4	pink and white roses with one pink rose offshoot	G3-6, 28, 31
5	two large pink roses with two rose offshoots	300-302
5a	the two large roses from FD5	303-311
6	pink poppies and lily of the valley	312-321
7	two open bloom pink roses and two smaller blooms	322-334
8	multi-colored roses	335-357
9	four large pink poppies with one closed poppy	358-375
10	a branch with two pink roses and one white rose	G3-41
11	large yellow roses with one white rose	G3-113, 115
11a	partial rose design from FD11	G3-173
12	white roses with one orange bloom (colors may vary)	G3-5, 187, 191
13	two orange roses and one pink rose	G3-17, 33
13a	two pink roses and one yellow rose (similar to FD13)	G3-18
14	pink roses with one orange rose and a cluster of white daisies at base of branch	376-385

RSP FD #	*Description of Pattern*	*Examples*
15	multi-colored roses with a small daisy cluster	386-390
16	multi-colored poppies (colors may vary)	391-397
17	large white poppies with multi-colored poppies	398-403
18	one white open poppy and one closed orange poppy	404-409; 411-422
18a-c	variations of FD18	406, 408, 410, 413, 419
19	a yellow, a white, and two pink roses	G3-38, 476
20	a pink and a yellow open bloom rose with one small pink bud	423-430
20a	the yellow rose from FD20	429
21	multi-colored mums and other flowers	G3-4
22	clusters of small multi-colored flowers	G3-37, 275, 276
23	white flower with a yellow center, yellow blossoms, and a yellow rose offshoot	431-439
23a	variation of FD23	G3-228
24	peach colored roses and a bud	G3-21, 257
25	Magnolias	440, 443-445, 447-456
25a	FD25 with one closed flower at top	441, 442, 446
26	dark pink and light pink lilies	457-472
27	one large pink rose with one pink bud	G3-59
28	dark pink and light pink roses	473-478
29	spray of pink lilies	G3-76
30	a pink rose with a small white flower	G3-92, 99, 381
30a	a pink rose with a small white flower and daisies	G3-137
31	Roses and Snowballs	479-495
31a	variation of FD31 with flowers in a glass bowl	496-507
32	a large light pink rose and a smaller white rose	G3-242, 251
33	pink poppies and a snowball	508-514
34	seven scattered flowers	515-519
35	one light pink and two dark pink roses	520-525
36	Reflecting Poppies and Daisies	526-531
37	one large dark pink rose, one white rose, and a shaggy pink blossom and bud	G3-119, 183
38	Reflecting Water Lilies	532-542
39	lilac clematis	543-551
40	bouquet of light and dark pink carnations	552-555
41	cluster of small lilac flowers	G3-136, 512
42	two large pale pink roses with three buds	G3-139
43	light and dark pink roses with two yellow roses and one light pink offshoot	G3-80
44	Hanging Basket	556-570
45	green-brown leaves with grain head	G3-144
46	one pink rose with small white leaves	G3-134
47	two white lilies with dogwood	571-579
48	Dogwood	580-582
49	Surreal Dogwood	583-586
49a-e	Surreal Dogwood variations	587-603
50	a large full bloom dark pink rose	G3-171
51	white bonnet shaped flowers with yellow pods	G3-172
52	a red rose, a pink rose, and a white rose with red center	604-613
53	dark pink, light pink and yellow roses	G3-178, 262, 265
54	bouquet of yellow tinted lilies and a bud	G3-214
55	white snowballs	614-618
56	daffodils	G3-185

RSP *FD #*	*Description of Pattern*	*Examples*
57	a large dark pink rose and bud with a pale pink rose	G3-224
58	large brown and green leaves with a cluster of yellow seed pods	G3-239
59	spray of small white flowers	G3-234, 236
60	one large white rose and one large pink rose	G3-237, 238
61	two large pink roses with a white leaf	G3-222
62	spray of small light and dark pink roses	G3-215, 335, 423
63	small yellow and white flowers with a lilac shadow	G3-219
64	two pale yellow roses with one offshoot	G3-235
65	two large pink roses on long stems with green leaves	G3-210
66	large green leaves on vine with small white flowers	G3-205, 254
67	cluster of white flowers with offshoots of a pair of orange and pink blooms	G3-208
68	two white flowers with one orange flower outlined in gold	G3-207
69	single daisy with laurel chain	G3-206
70	large pink roses and a bud	G3-197
71	one large white spider mum, one dark pink open rose, and a dark pink rose offshoot	G3-135, 226
72	one light pink and one dark pink rose with two small buds and two blooms extending from center	G3-188
73	a pink and a white tulip	G3-174, 246, 325
74	a large cluster of multi-colored roses and green leaves on a branch	G3-148
75	three pink roses with green leaves	G3-149
76	spray of shaggy pink roses	G3-36, 168
77	white blossoms with a lavender tint	G3-155, 268
78	a large white and a large pink open petal blossom with a closed white bloom at top and a small white flower at bottom	G3-516
79	Calla Lily	619-624
80	cluster of large open pink-orange blooms	G3-255, 341
81	white poppies with a pink tint	G3-286, 366
82	two large white blossoms with yellow centers	G3-288
83	large open bloom white flowers	G3-289
84	cluster of purple and white flowers	G3-324
85	Lily of the Valley	625-634
85a	Lily of the Valley molded design	635-638
86	a pink rose spray with an offshoot of two entwined buds and green leaves	639-644
86a	spray of three pink roses and one offshoot	G3-457
86b	spray of large pink roses with an offshoot of three blooms with green leaves	G3-478
87	evergreen branch	G3-294
88	cluster of white roses	645-650
89	cluster of pink and white tulips	G3-292
90	Sitting Basket	651-654
91	spray of pink flowers with one large white flower	655-662
92	cluster of purple and small white flowers	G3-243, 363
93	large pink flowers with two buds	G3-415
94	cluster of red and white roses	G3-418
95	Canterbury Bells	663-667
96	pink and white spider mums	G3-461
97	Dogwood and Pine	668-678
98	one light pink and two dark pink roses with a dark pink rose offshoot	G3-305
98a	same transfer as FD98, except offshoot is a bud rather than a full rose	G3-305
99	spray of pink and white carnations	G3-479
100	a dark pink and a light pink rose with a light pink rose offshoot	G3-480

Creative Artists' Signatures

These four photographs illustrate details of R.S. Prussia floral transfers. Signatures are shown of the artisans who either designed the mold or the art work for the original transfer. Kolb, Klett, and Rein were mold makers; Happ was a design painter.

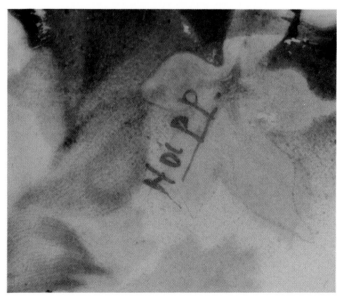

R.S. Prussia Decoration Subjects

Items are listed by plate numbers used in this book.

Index to R.S. Prussia Objects